Teacher Guide

LEVEL G

VOCABULARY

word meaning, pronunciation, prefixes, suffixes, synonyms, antonyms, and fun!

in Action

LOYOLA PRESS.

Chicago

LOYOLA PRESS.

3441 N. Ashland Avenue
Chicago, Illinois 60657
(800) 621-1008
www.loyolapress.com

Cover & Interior Art: Anni Betts
Cover Design: Judine O'Shea
Interior Design: Kathy Greenholdt

Manufactured in the United States of America.

ISBN-10: 0-8294-2780-5

ISBN-13: 978-0-8294-2780-6

10 11 12 13 14 15 16 17 Hess 10 9 8 6 7 5 4 3 2 1

VISIT
www.vocabularyinaction.com
ACCESS CODE: **VTB-8994**

Contents

This key shows the meanings of the abbreviations and symbols used throughout the book.

Some English words have more than one possible pronunciation. This book gives only one pronunciation per word, except when different pronunciations indicate different parts of speech. For example, when the word *relay* is used as a noun, it is pronounced rē´ lā; as a verb, the word is pronounced rə lā´.

Parts of Speech

adj.	adjective	*int.*	interjection	*prep.*	preposition
adv.	adverb	*n.*	noun	*part.*	participle
				v.	verb

Vowels

ā	tape	ə	about, circus	ôr	torn
a	map	ī	kite	oi	noise
âr	stare	i	win	ou	foul
ä	car, father	ō	toe	o͞o	soon
ē	meet	o	mop	o͝o	book
e	kept	ô	law	u	tug

Consonants

ch	check	ŋ	rang	y	yellow
g	girl	th	thimble	zh	treasure
j	jam	th	that	sh	shelf

Stress

The accent mark follows the syllable receiving the major stress, such as in the word *plaster* (plas´ tər).

Introduction

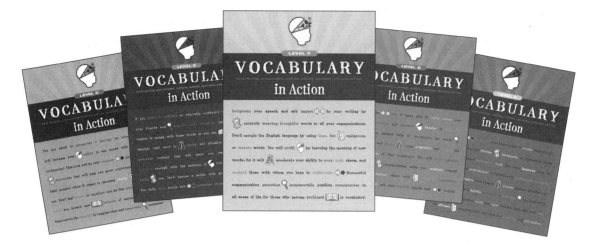

Vocabulary in Action is the premier vocabulary development program that increases students' literacy skills and improves test scores.

Researchers and educators agree that vocabulary development is essential in learning how to communicate effectively through listening, speaking, reading, and writing. The National Reading Panel (2000) has identified vocabulary as one of the five areas that increase students' reading ability. After the third grade, reading difficulties are often attributed to a vocabulary deficit—an inability to understand word meaning.

Vocabulary in Action offers the following elements to help students develop this critical literacy skill:

- Flexible leveling and student placement for individualized instruction

- Words that were researched and selected specifically for frequency, occurrence, and relevance to assessment and everyday life

- Intentional, direct instruction focused on words and their meanings, usage, and relationships to other words

- Repeated word appearance in a variety of contexts for extensive exposure and practice with literal and figurative meanings

- Application of new vocabulary skills through practice exercises, assessments, and standardized test preparation opportunities

Program Overview

Each Student Book includes

- **Program Pretest** to identify level of understanding

- **Research-based Word Lists** selected for frequency, occurrence, and relevance to assessment

- **One Hundred or More Related Words** including synonyms and antonyms

- **Word Pronunciations, Meanings, and Identifications of Parts of Speech**

- **At Least a Dozen Activities per Chapter,** including activities for words in context, word meaning, word usage, related words, and word building

- **Challenge Words and Activities**

- **Fun with Words** activities for additional practice

- **Test-Taking Tips** section covering test-taking skills, testing formats, and study of testing vocabulary including classic roots, prefixes, and suffixes

- **Special Features** for etymology, mnemonic devices, historical facts, word trivia, and word origin

- **Notable Quotes** that show words in context

- **Chapter Review Assessments** for multiple chapters

- **Program Posttest** to determine overall growth

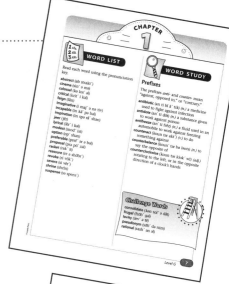

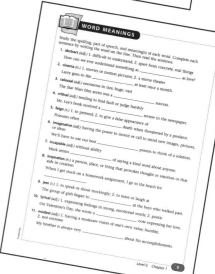

Total Vocabulary Word Count by Level

LEVEL	WORDS TO KNOW	ADDITIONAL WORDS
D	150	over 100
E	225	over 150
F, G, H	375	over 200

Each Teacher Guide includes

- **Annotated Guide** similar to the student book for easy correction

- **Additional Games and Activities** for a variety of groupings, learning styles, multiple intelligences, and levels of proficiency in English

- **Suggestions for Guided and Independent Practice**

- **Academic Language Practice** with games and activities, including work with classic roots

- **Icons** for easy identification

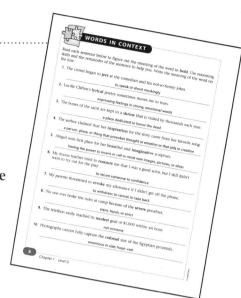

The *Vocabulary in Action* Web site includes

- Assessments

- Pretests and Reviews

- Word Lists and Definitions

- Vocabulary Games

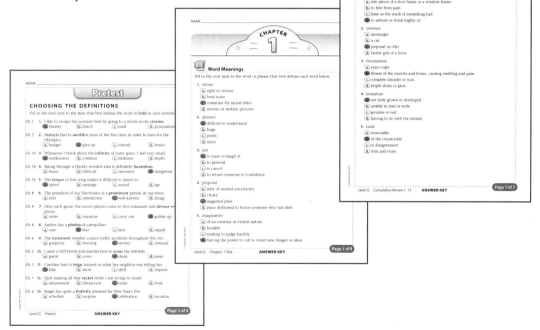

www.vocabularyinaction.com

How to Implement This Program

With *Vocabulary in Action*, it is easy to differentiate instruction to meet the needs of all students.

Student Placement

Use the following chart to help determine the book most appropriate for each individual student. Differences in level include word difficulty, sentence complexity, and ideas presented in context. In addition to the chart, consider a student's achievement level on any pretest that you give. Adjust books based on a student's achievement on a pretest and other vocabulary assignments, his or her ability to retain new information, and the student's overall work ethic and interest level.

Placement Levels

Typical Grade-Level Assignments		Accelerated Grade-Level Assignments	
LEVEL	GRADE	LEVEL	GRADE
D	4	D	3
E	5	E	4
F	6	F	5
G	7	G	6
H	8	H	7

To Begin

At the beginning of the year, choose a book for each student based on the above criteria. Have each student take the program pretest in his or her book. Avoid timing the test. Give students enough time to complete the test thoughtfully and with confidence. After grading the test and noting student achievement levels, make book adjustments if necessary.

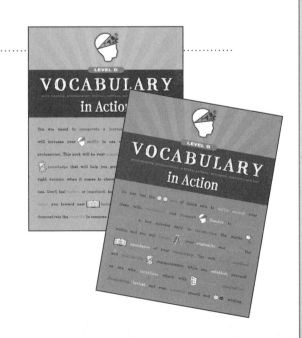

Work Through the Chapters

Follow these steps to implement each chapter.

1. **Chapter opener:** Have students work with partners, in small groups, or with you to read aloud each word in the **Word List.** Check pronunciation and discuss the definition of each word, having students find the words in a dictionary if you have time. Have students review the **Word Study** section. Introduce the **Challenge Words** in the same way as the Word List. Then have students remove the page and complete the back side.

2. **Chapter pages:** Based on students' confidence and ability, assign students to complete chapter activities independently, with you, with peers, or as homework. Students should complete activities for Words in Context, Word Meanings, Use Your Vocabulary, Word Learning, Synonyms, Antonyms, Word Study, Challenge Words, and Fun with Words. Provide support through modeling and discussion. Here are some approaches:

   - Teacher presents and completes a page with students during the first 10 or 15 minutes of each reading or language arts session. Pages are reviewed simultaneously as guided practice.

   - Students complete chapter pages in class after other reading or language arts assignments are complete. Pages are collected and reviewed after class.

   - Students complete chapter pages as homework assignments, one page per night. Pages are collected and reviewed after completion.

3. **Reteaching/additional practice:** Monitor student progress on a regular basis. If students need additional practice, use the **Games & Activities** on pages 189–194 of this guide or the **Teacher Activities** on pages 195–196.

4. **Standardized test preparation:** At least one month prior to standardized testing, work with students to complete pages 183–184.

5. **Chapter reviews:** After completing every three chapters, administer the Chapter Review to note students' progress and to identify difficult words.

6. **Assessment:** Have students complete a formal assessment after each chapter. Visit **www.vocabularyinaction.com** and access the assessment with this code: **VTB-8994.** You can also access a **Pretest** and **Review.**

Sample Yearly Plan for Level G

Following is one way to implement *Vocabulary in Action* for Level G.

WEEK	STUDENT BOOK	RELATED ACTIVITIES	
1	Pretest		
2–3	Chapter 1	Games & Activities (pp. 189–194) Teacher Activities (pp. 195–196)	Chapter 1 Assessment
4–5	Chapter 2	Games & Activities (pp. 189–194) Teacher Activities (pp. 195–196)	Chapter 2 Assessment
6–7	Chapter 3	Games & Activities (pp. 189–194) Teacher Activities (pp. 195–196)	Chapter 3 Assessment
8	Review Chapters 1–3	Online Games (www.vocabularyinaction.com) Cumulative Review	
9–10	Chapter 4	Games & Activities (pp. 189–194) Teacher Activities (pp. 195–196)	Chapter 4 Assessment
11–12	Chapter 5	Games & Activities (pp. 189–194) Teacher Activities (pp. 195–196)	Chapter 5 Assessment
13–14	Chapter 6	Games & Activities (pp. 189–194) Teacher Activities (pp. 195–196)	Chapter 6 Assessment
15	Review Chapters 4–6	Online Games (www.vocabularyinaction.com) Cumulative Review	
16–17	Chapter 7	Games & Activities (pp. 189–194) Teacher Activities (pp. 195–196)	Chapter 7 Assessment
18–19	Chapter 8	Games & Activities (pp. 189–194) Teacher Activities (pp. 195–196)	Chapter 8 Assessment
20–21	Chapter 9	Games & Activities (pp. 189–194) Teacher Activities (pp. 195–196)	Chapter 9 Assessment
22	Review Chapters 7–9	Online Games (www.vocabularyinaction.com) Cumulative Review	
23	Chapter 10	Games & Activities (pp. 189–194) Teacher Activities (pp. 195–196)	Chapter 10 Assessment
24–25	Chapter 11	Games & Activities (pp. 189–194) Teacher Activities (pp. 195–196)	Chapter 11 Assessment
26–27	Chapter 12	Games & Activities (pp. 189–194) Teacher Activities (pp. 195–196)	Chapter 12 Assessment
28	Review Chapters 10–12	Online Games (www.vocabularyinaction.com) Cumulative Review	
29	Chapter 13	Games & Activities (pp. 189–194) Teacher Activities (pp. 195–196)	Chapter 13 Assessment
30–31	Chapter 14	Games & Activities (pp. 189–194) Teacher Activities (pp. 195–196)	Chapter 14 Assessment
32–33	Chapter 15	Games & Activities (pp. 189–194) Teacher Activities (pp. 195–196)	Chapter 15 Assessment
34	Review Chapters 13–15	Online Games (www.vocabularyinaction.com) Cumulative Review	
35	Posttest		

Pretest

This test contains some of the words you will find in this book. It will give you an idea of the kinds of words you will study. When you have completed all the chapters, the Posttest will measure what you have learned.

Choosing the Definitions

Fill in the bubble next to the item that best defines the boldface word in each sentence.

Ch. 3 **1.** The cancellation of the game **provoked** an angry response from the fans.
    (a.) subdued   (b.) shouted   (c.) stirred up   (d.) resulted from

Ch. 8 **2.** Carlos thought the decision was unfair, but he kept his **grievance** to himself.
    (a.) sadness   (b.) doubts   (c.) complaint   (d.) excitement

Ch. 5 **3.** The siren made the child **quake** with fear.
    (a.) bark   (b.) tremble   (c.) whimper   (d.) bite

Ch. 4 **4.** A group of citizens **ridiculed** the new statue on the village square.
    (a.) admired   (b.) ruined   (c.) shaped   (d.) laughed at

Ch. 4 **5.** Conflicting evidence can **mystify** a detective.
    (a.) condemn   (b.) confuse   (c.) frighten   (d.) please

Ch. 2 **6.** Lou's next-door neighbor was once a **renowned** athlete.
    (a.) famous   (b.) bungling   (c.) injured   (d.) skillful

Ch. 5 **7.** Ian listened thoughtfully, but decided he couldn't **subscribe** to the group's beliefs.
    (a.) agree with   (b.) investigate   (c.) be unsure of   (d.) write about

Ch. 10 **8.** The firefighters removed the kitten from its **precarious** position.
    (a.) preferred   (b.) unsafe   (c.) awkward   (d.) comfortable

Ch. 1 **9.** Sharon has the **option** of playing soccer or running track.
    (a.) time   (b.) speed   (c.) opinion   (d.) choice

Ch. 6 **10.** The crew worked together to **inflate** the hot-air balloon.
    (a.) lower   (b.) measure   (c.) expand   (d.) pop

Ch. 15 **11.** The veterinarian said the stray dog was an **immature** collie.
    (a.) playful   (b.) nervous   (c.) young   (d.) hungry

Ch. 6 **12.** The color guard arrived and **unfurled** the flag.
    (a.) unrolled   (b.) unlocked   (c.) folded   (d.) raised

Ch. 6 **13.** For help with the computer, I will **refer** you to the librarian.
   (a.) talk about   (b.) escort   (c.) remember   **(d.) direct**

Ch. 7 **14.** The rural dirt road led us to a **desolate** location.
   (a.) beautiful   **(b.) deserted**   (c.) dry   (d.) comforting

Ch. 5 **15.** Marty vowed to **defy** his brother's prediction that he would fail.
   (a.) repeat   (b.) fulfill   **(c.) challenge**   (d.) obey

Ch. 7 **16.** It was hard to see through the thick green **foliage.**
   (a.) leaves   (b.) fabric   (c.) window   (d.) lawn

Ch. 2 **17.** The runner's **resolve** to finish the marathon keeps her going.
   (a.) determination (b.) endurance   (c.) flexibility   (d.) race

Ch. 3 **18.** A **nebulous** shape emerged from the mist.
   (a.) frightening   **(b.) indistinct**   (c.) huge   (d.) triangular

Ch. 7 **19.** Jared offered to **sacrifice** his allowance for the charity drive.
   (a.) spend   **(b.) give up**   (c.) save   (d.) pack up

Ch. 8 **20.** The whole family worked together on the vacation **agenda.**
   (a.) reservations   (b.) packing   (c.) bill   **(d.) schedule**

Ch. 2 **21.** Alison makes **frequent** trips to her grandmother's house.
   (a.) long   (b.) occasional   **(c.) often**   (d.) low-cost

Ch. 8 **22.** Living in **penury** while he looked for a job taught Willie compassion.
   (a.) wealth   (b.) prison   (c.) motels   **(d.) poverty**

Ch. 8 **23.** Peter Jennings was a **prominent** news reporter.
   (a.) talented   **(b.) well-known**   (c.) curious   (d.) dedicated

Ch. 4 **24.** When the phone rang, Bert pressed the **mute** button on the remote control.
   (a.) power   (b.) rewind   (c.) pause   **(d.) quiet**

Ch. 1 **25.** After Wendy heard the rumor, she hurried to **reassure** her friend.
   (a.) help again   **(b.) comfort**   (c.) accompany   (d.) abandon

Ch. 9 **26.** It was just a **coincidence** that both girls wore the same outfit.
   (a.) chance event (b.) story   (c.) collision   (d.) quick decision

Ch. 9 **27.** We thought he was a police officer, but he was really an **impostor.**
   (a.) doctor   (b.) model   **(c.) pretender**   (d.) soldier

Ch. 9 **28.** Dad **gravely** examined the note from the principal.
   (a.) tearfully   (b.) politely   **(c.) seriously**   (d.) quickly

Ch. 9 **29.** The additional speaker **prolonged** the ceremony.
    (a.) conducted   (b.) planned   (c.) shortened   **(d.) lengthened**

Ch. 6 **30.** The ice on the sidewalk made walking **treacherous**.
    (a.) hazardous   (b.) secure   (c.) slippery   (d.) exciting

Ch. 10 **31.** The art teacher says we **consume** the supplies too quickly.
    (a.) purchase   **(b.) use up**   (c.) arrange   (d.) paint

Ch. 12 **32.** The leak was caused by a **rupture** in the plumbing system.
    (a.) clog   (b.) repair   (c.) curve   **(d.) break**

Ch. 1 **33.** The judge said the punishment was too **severe** for the minor crime.
    (a.) long   (b.) easy   **(c.) harsh**   (d.) complicated

Ch. 10 **34.** The skaters waited eagerly for **feedback** from the judges.
    (a.) payment   **(b.) reaction**   (c.) sorrow   (d.) argument

Ch. 3 **35.** Going out into the cold is unpleasant, but the **alternative** is boring.
    (a.) choice   (b.) beginning   (c.) answer   (d.) warmth

Ch. 6 **36.** A **surge** of electricity damaged the computer.
    (a.) outage   (b.) lack   (c.) lightning   **(d.) torrent**

Ch. 10 **37.** The magician startled the audience with a convincing **illusion**.
    (a.) lie   (b.) true story   **(c.) false image**   (d.) light

Ch. 7 **38.** The community gathered together to **reap** their sick neighbor's crop.
    (a.) destroy   (b.) eat   (c.) plant   **(d.) harvest**

Ch. 2 **39.** Dad and Phil **scoured** the frying pans.
    (a.) dirtied   **(b.) scrubbed**   (c.) heated   (d.) dropped

Ch. 10 **40.** Matt is upset when his other chores cause him to **neglect** the garden.
    (a.) plant   (b.) fertilize   **(c.) ignore**   (d.) weed

Ch. 1 **41.** Scott **feigned** sleep when Mom asked him to put out the trash.
    (a.) pretended   (b.) went to   (c.) caused   (d.) lost

Ch. 3 **42.** Kim likes to perform, but she hopes she won't **bungle** the new song.
    (a.) mess up   (b.) remember   (c.) lose her voice   (d.) have to sing

Ch. 10 **43.** The inexperienced **recruit** worked hard to learn the rules quickly.
    (a.) tutor   (b.) volunteer   **(c.) new member**   (d.) firefighter

Ch. 10 **44.** Even though many players have graduated, the coach hopes to **retain** the championship title this year.
    (a.) lose out   (b.) announce   (c.) try for   **(d.) keep**

Ch. 5 45. Mac asked for extra help because he was **bewildered** by algebra.
a. angered   **b. confused**   c. thrilled   d. harmed

Ch. 14 46. Ivy covered the old building's **exterior** walls.
a. decorated   **b. outside**   c. decaying   d. unnecessary

Ch. 10 47. Ruth's everyday actions are a **testament** to her beliefs.
a. explanation   b. age   c. denial   **d. statement**

Ch. 4 48. A city **ordinance** forbids parking on the street on snowy days.
a. council   b. light   **c. law**   d. highway

Ch. 11 49. The group planned to **append** the new information to their report.
a. add   b. send   c. research   d. praise

Ch. 7 50. The cuffs of Jay's jeans were entangled in a **bramble** in the berry patch.
a. trap   b. tree branch   **c. thorny shrub**   d. web

Ch. 14 51. The rebels plotted to **usurp** the governor's power.
a. aid   **b. seize**   c. vote for   d. predict

Ch. 11 52. The new catcher's **initiation** came in the game against the first-place team.
a. background   b. uniform   **c. beginning**   d. triumph

Ch. 10 53. The crew set up huge speakers to **amplify** the band's music.
a. make louder   b. help play   c. turn down   d. listen to

Ch. 2 54. The actor was so **egotistical** he didn't talk about anything but himself.
a. busy   **b. vain**   c. noisy   d. tired

Ch. 11 55. Daria's mother encouraged her to choose a **practical** pair of shoes.
a. athletic   b. unattractive   c. comfortable   **d. useful**

Ch. 11 56. The shareholders were pleased when the company's **revenue** increased.
a. product   **b. income**   c. employees   d. taxes

Ch. 4 57. It can be as much fun to watch an **amateur** game as a major league game.
a. expert   b. exciting   c. baseball   **d. nonprofessional**

Ch. 11 58. The hard work paid off for my **studious** neighbor.
a. strong   b. teenage   **c. scholarly**   d. overworked

Ch. 15 59. At the end of the ride, Sandy **galloped** the horse toward home.
a. pointed   **b. sped**   c. led   d. walked

Ch. 5 60. You need all the facts to make a **logical** decision.
a. bad   b. favorite   c. hard   **d. sensible**

Ch. 11 **61.** Let's wrap the coins and **tally** the rolls of quarters.
  a. deposit   **b.** unroll   **c.** spend   **d.** count

Ch. 14 **62.** Is that just a strange-looking stone, or is it an **authentic** fossil?
  a. ancient   **b.** fake   **c.** genuine   **d.** dated

Ch. 1 **63.** The group considered Vita's **imaginative** idea.
  a. creative   **b.** first   **c.** boring   **d.** stale

Ch. 12 **64.** Most community activities occur in the **nucleus** of our town.
  a. outskirts   **b.** city hall   **c.** park   **d.** center

Ch. 12 **65.** The class looked forward to their opportunity to **probe** the ancient ruins.
  a. map   **b.** protect   **c.** explore   **d.** dig up

Ch. 8 **66.** We can earn extra **privileges** by doing extra chores.
  a. special advantages   **b.** points   **c.** days off   **d.** spending money

Ch. 12 **67.** The new invention will **revolutionize** the industry.
  a. take over   **b.** greatly change   **c.** ruin   **d.** improve

Ch. 13 **68.** The new cashier didn't know how to **cope** with the angry customer.
  a. handle   **b.** argue   **c.** agree   **d.** leave

Ch. 3 **69.** The group will not **condemn** him for one small mistake.
  a. dismiss   **b.** congratulate   **c.** forgive   **d.** denounce

Ch. 13 **70.** The new office building is at the **junction** of two major highways.
  a. edge   **b.** end   **c.** joining   **d.** beginning

Ch. 13 **71.** Even though they liked it, Barb's friends **needled** her about her new haircut.
  a. praised   **b.** teased   **c.** poked   **d.** asked

Ch. 3 **72.** Dad was **irate** when he discovered what we had done.
  a. thrilled   **b.** angry   **c.** scared   **d.** amused

Ch. 13 **73.** Stella's **primary** reason for taking dance lessons was to get exercise.
  a. worst   **b.** last   **c.** simplest   **d.** first

Ch. 13 **74.** The thin jacket is warm because it is made from **synthetic** material.
  a. scratchy   **b.** natural   **c.** manufactured   **d.** shiny

Ch. 9 **75.** Theo was embarrassed when everyone laughed at his **blunder.**
  a. error   **b.** joke   **c.** speech   **d.** singing

Ch. 13 **76.** The band made only one **minor** mistake during the show.
  a. small   **b.** noticeable   **c.** careless   **d.** huge

Ch. 14 77. The crowd cheered as the explorers set off on the **hazardous** journey.
  (a.) planned   (b.) lengthy   (c.) dangerous   (d.) exciting

Ch. 5 78. The purpose of the mission was **cloaked** in secrecy.
  (a.) discussed   (b.) concealed   (c.) enjoyed   (d.) televised

Ch. 14 79. It was hard to imagine that the twins could leave the house in **shambles**.
  (a.) good order   (b.) the city   (c.) the country   (d.) messy condition

Ch. 15 80. The important package was brought by the **courier**.
  (a.) wind   (b.) messenger   (c.) pony   (d.) secretary

Ch. 2 81. Prior to the meeting, we all had dinner together.
  (a.) during   (b.) after   (c.) below   (d.) before

Ch. 15 82. To get ready for the competition, Thora put the **quiver** over her shoulder.
  (a.) arrow case   (b.) backpack   (c.) wool blanket   (d.) cloak

Ch. 12 83. The air was filled with thick white **fumes**.
  (a.) dust particles   (b.) storm clouds   (c.) feathers   (d.) smoke

Ch. 15 84. A group of **unruly** children visited the museum.
  (a.) polite   (b.) intelligent   (c.) uncontrollable   (d.) young

Ch. 12 85. To make the decoration, you'll need a long, wooden **cylinder**.
  (a.) splinter   (b.) wand   (c.) branch   (d.) tube

Ch. 15 86. The song was easier to sing after the director changed the **tempo**.
  (a.) words   (b.) tune   (c.) speed   (d.) theme

Ch. 6 87. I know it's silly, but I have a **phobia** about bugs.
  (a.) collection   (b.) fear   (c.) book   (d.) love

Ch. 12 88. The plan for school uniforms met with **resistance** at first.
  (a.) open arms   (b.) forgetfulness   (c.) refusal   (d.) forgiveness

Ch. 13 89. The planets in our solar system **revolve** around the sun.
  (a.) orbit   (b.) wander   (c.) explode   (d.) disappear

Ch. 8 90. Leon wondered why everyone **grimaced** at his joke.
  (a.) laughed out loud   (b.) walked away from   (c.) made a face   (d.) clapped

CHAPTER 1

WORD LIST

Read each word using the pronunciation key.

abstract (ab strakt´)
cinema (sin´ ə mə)
colossal (kə los´ əl)
critical (krit´ i kəl)
feign (fān)
imaginative (i maj´ ə nə tiv)
incapable (in kā´ pə bəl)
inspiration (in spə rā´ shən)
jeer (jēr)
lyrical (lēr´ i kəl)
modest (mod´ ist)
option (op´ shən)
preferable (pref´ ər ə bəl)
proposal (prə pō´ zəl)
racket (rak´ it)
reassure (re ə sho͝or´)
revoke (ri vōk´)
severe (si vēr´)
shrine (shrīn)
suspense (sə spens´)

WORD STUDY

Prefixes

The prefixes *anti-* and *counter-* mean "against, opposed to," or "contrary."

antibiotic (an ti bī ä´ tik) *(n.)* a medicine used to fight against infection
antidote (an´ ti dōt) *(n.)* a substance given to work against poison
antifreeze (an´ ti frēz) *(n.)* a fluid used in an automobile to work against freezing
counteract (koun tər akt´) *(v.)* to do something against
counterbalance (koun´ tər ba lənts) *(n.)* to say the opposite of
counterclockwise (koun tər klok´ wī) *(adj.)* rotating to the left, or in the opposite direction of a clock's hands

Challenge Words

consolidate (kən sol´ ə dāt)
frugal (fro͞o´ gəl)
levity (lev´ ə tē)
pseudonym (so͞o´ də nim)
rational (rash´ ən əl)

■ **TEACHER TIP:** See page ix for suggestions on how to use this page.

WORDS IN CONTEXT

Read each sentence below to figure out the meaning of the word in **bold**. Use reasoning skills and the remainder of the sentence to help you. Write the meaning of the word on the line.

1. The crowd began to **jeer** at the comedian and his not-so-funny jokes.

    to speak or shout mockingly

2. Lucille Clifton's **lyrical** poetry sometimes moves me to tears.

    expressing feelings in strong, emotional words

3. The bones of the saint are kept in a **shrine** that is visited by thousands each year.

    a place dedicated to honor the dead

4. The author claimed that her **inspiration** for the story came from her favorite song.

    a person, place, or thing that provokes thought or emotion or that aids in creation

5. Abigail won first place for her beautiful and **imaginative** sculpture.

    having the power to invent or call to mind new images, pictures, or ideas

6. My drama teacher tried to **reassure** me that I was a good actor, but I still didn't want to try out for the play.

    to return someone to confidence

7. My parents threatened to **revoke** my allowance if I didn't get off the phone.

    to withdraw; to cancel; to take back

8. No one ever broke the rules at camp because of the **severe** penalties.

    stern, harsh, or strict

9. The telethon easily reached its **modest** goal of $1,000 within an hour.

    not extreme

10. Photographs cannot fully capture the **colossal** size of the Egyptian pyramids.

    enormous in size; huge; vast

WORD MEANINGS

Study the spelling, part of speech, and meaning(s) of each word. Complete each sentence by writing the word on the line. Then read the sentence.

1. **abstract** *(adj.)* 1. difficult to understand; 2. apart from concrete, real things

   How can we ever understand something as _____abstract_____ as love?

2. **cinema** *(n.)* 1. movies or motion pictures; 2. a movie theater

   Larry goes to the _____cinema_____ at least once a month.

3. **colossal** *(adj.)* enormous in size; huge; vast

   The *Star Wars* film series was a _____colossal_____ success.

4. **critical** *(adj.)* tending to find fault or judge harshly

   Mr. Lee's book received a _____critical_____ review in the newspaper.

5. **feign** *(v.)* 1. to pretend; 2. to give a false appearance of

   Opossums often _____feign_____ death when threatened by a predator.

6. **imaginative** *(adj.)* having the power to invent or call to mind new images, pictures, or ideas

   We'll have to use our best _____imaginative_____ powers to think of a solution.

7. **incapable** *(adj.)* without ability

   Mark seems _____incapable_____ of saying a kind word about anyone.

8. **inspiration** *(n.)* a person, place, or thing that provokes thought or emotion or that aids in creation

   When I get stuck on a homework assignment, I go to the beach for _____inspiration_____.

9. **jeer** *(v.)* 1. to speak or shout mockingly; 2. to tease or laugh at

   The group of girls began to _____jeer_____ at the boys who walked past.

10. **lyrical** *(adj.)* 1. expressing feelings in strong, emotional words; 2. poetic

    On Valentine's Day, she wrote a _____lyrical_____ note expressing her love.

11. **modest** *(adj.)* 1. having a moderate vision of one's own value; humble; 2. not extreme

    My brother is always very _____modest_____ about his accomplishments.

12. **option** *(n.)* choice or the right to choose

    If you don't like it, you always have the _____ option _____ to leave.

13. **preferable** *(adj.)* more desirable

    I'd find it _____ preferable _____ to meet at five o'clock instead of six.

14. **proposal** *(n.)* 1. a suggested plan or scheme; 2. the act of suggesting something

    You can present your _____ proposal _____ to the team.

15. **racket** *(n.)* 1. a piece of sports equipment with a handle and a round or an oval frame with tightly laced strings, used to hit a ball; 2. a loud noise; 3. an illegal business

    She could hit the ball much faster with the new tennis _____ racket _____.

16. **reassure** *(v.)* to return someone to confidence

    I _____ reassure _____ you that no one wants to take your property.

17. **revoke** *(v.)* 1. to withdraw; 2. to cancel

    If you cause a bad accident, the state may _____ revoke _____ your driver's license.

18. **severe** *(adj.)* 1. stern, harsh, or strict; 2. of an extreme, sharp, or violent nature

    Our teacher gave us a _____ severe _____ lecture about pulling fire alarms.

19. **shrine** *(n.)* 1. a place or container for sacred relics; 2. a place dedicated to honor someone who has died

    The people had built a _____ shrine _____ to the former emperor.

20. **suspense** *(n.)* 1. the state of being anxious as a result of uncertainty; 2. the state of mental uncertainty; indecision

    As we waited for her decision, the _____ suspense _____ was unbearable.

Notable Quotes

"I could never tell where **inspiration** begins and impulse leaves off. I suppose the answer is in the outcome. If your hunch proves a good one, you were inspired; if it proves bad, you are guilty of yielding to thoughtless impulse."

—Beryl Markham (1902–1986), British-born Kenyan author

Use Your Vocabulary

Choose the word from the Word List that best completes each sentence. Write the word on the line. You may use the plural form of nouns and the past tense of verbs if necessary.

Our whole town went to the __1__ last night for a special showing of movies by local filmmakers. Frankly, staying at home with my computer games seemed __2__ to sitting through all of those movies. But my mother did not give me the __3__ of staying home. My teacher, Ms. Kushner, was presenting her film. I reminded my mother that I was __4__ of staying awake when I was bored. She told me not to be foolish and to at least __5__ interest, out of respect for Ms. Kushner.

"Why is this such a(n) __6__ event, anyway? It's just a couple of dumb movies," I grumbled. My mother __7__ me that the movies would not be dumb. I offered to wash dishes for a week if she'd let me stay home, but she rejected my __8__ with a(n) __9__ look. When she threatened to __10__ my TV privileges for a month, I agreed to go.

The first film told the story of a gambling __11__ run by a dangerous mobster. I was in terrible __12__ the whole time, wondering whether the clever detective would catch the criminals. Mr. Gafer, who made the film, said that his __13__ came from 20 years of service as a police officer.

The second movie was so __14__ and confusing that I still don't know what it was about. The audience began to __15__ at a scene in which a penguin crashed a pickup truck. I joined the booing as well, but my father told me not to be so __16__ of someone's hard work, so I stopped. He said that the film had clearly been made by a very __17__ and creative person.

The best movie was Ms. Kushner's. It was about three boys who built a(n) __18__ to honor the baseball legend Jackie Robinson. The __19__ dialogue made me laugh, cry, and gasp with surprise.

Afterwards, Ms. Kushner was too __20__ to believe that her movie was the best I'd ever seen.

1. _____ cinema

2. _____ preferable

3. _____ option

4. _____ incapable

5. _____ feign

6. _____ colossal

7. _____ reassured

8. _____ proposal

9. _____ severe

10. _____ revoke

11. _____ racket

12. _____ suspense

13. _____ inspiration

14. _____ abstract

15. _____ jeer

16. _____ critical

17. _____ imaginative

18. _____ shrine

19. _____ lyrical

20. _____ modest

SYNONYMS

Synonyms are words that have the same or nearly the same meanings.

Part 1 Choose the word from the box that is the best synonym for each group of words. Write the word on the line.

cinema	critical	imaginative	inspiration
colossal	feign	incapable	suspense

1. nagging, faultfinding _____ critical

2. influence, stimulus, motivation _____ inspiration

3. uncertainty, tension, anxiety _____ suspense

4. imitate, fake, simulate _____ feign

5. unfit, inadequate, unable, incompetent _____ incapable

6. movies, film, theater _____ cinema

7. gigantic, immense, massive _____ colossal

8. creative, inventive, clever _____ imaginative

Part 2 Replace the underlined word with a word from the box that means the same or almost the same. Write your answer on the line.

abstract	racket	modest	severe
jeer	proposal	reassure	

9. She felt so bad, I was unable to <u>encourage</u> her. _____ reassure

10. If they <u>laugh</u> at you, don't listen to them. _____ jeer

11. There was a huge <u>uproar</u> when the two began to fight. _____ racket

12. The report was filled with many <u>confusing</u> ideas. _____ abstract

13. They suggested a <u>moderate</u> solution to the problem. _____ modest

14. Improper lifting can lead to <u>terrible</u> back pain. _____ severe

15. The group came up with a clever <u>idea</u> for the spring dance. _____ proposal

ANTONYMS

Antonyms are words that have opposite or nearly opposite meanings.

Part 1 Choose the word from the box that is the best antonym for each group of words. Write the word on the line.

abstract	colossal	incapable	modest	reassure

1. boastful, showy, prideful   _____modest_____

2. unnerve, discourage   _____reassure_____

3. small, tiny, minute   _____colossal_____

4. clear, obvious, uncomplicated   _____abstract_____

5. able, competent, effective   _____incapable_____

Part 2 Replace the underlined word with a word from the box that means the opposite or almost the opposite. Write your answer on the line.

critical	revoke	severe	racket	jeer

6. The school has placed <u>gentle</u> restrictions on lunchtime behavior.
   _____severe_____

7. After the first act, the audience began to <u>applaud</u> loudly. _____jeer_____

8. Raffi cast a <u>favorable</u> glance in my direction. _____critical_____

9. The committee has the power to <u>grant</u> any privileges. _____revoke_____

10. After we announced our decision, there was a great <u>silence</u>. _____racket_____

Vocabulary in Action

Abstract art is sometimes called nonfigurative or nonrepresentational art. This is because abstract art does not depict objects in the natural world. You won't usually see recognizable forms, such as people, animals, or mountains, in an abstract painting. Abstract art emphasizes color and form. But making abstract art is more difficult than it looks. In fact, 20th-century Russian painter Wassily Kandinsky wrote, "Of all the arts, abstract painting is the most difficult. It demands that you know how to draw well, that you have a heightened sensitivity for composition and for colors, and that you be a true poet. This last is essential."

WORD STUDY

Prefixes Use the words in the box to complete the following sentences.

antibiotic	antifreeze	counteract
antidote	counterbalance	counterclockwise

1. She hoped that her own cheerfulness would _____counteract_____ her friend's gloom.

2. The circle of dancers turned _____counterclockwise_____.

3. When I had strep throat, my doctor prescribed a(n) _____antibiotic_____.

4. When we go hiking, we bring a(n) _____antidote_____ for snakebite.

5. I must _____counterbalance_____ your argument with my opposing viewpoint.

6. At the beginning of each winter, my father buys a bottle of _____antifreeze_____ for the car.

Vocabulary in Action

English novelist Mary Ann (Marian) Evans (1819–1880) was one of the leading English novelists of the Victorian era. She wrote 7 novels, 11 books of poetry, and a number of nonfiction works.

Have you heard of her? If not, perhaps it is because Evans published all her work using a **pseudonym**—a pen name. Her pseudonym was George Eliot.

Evans, or Eliot, was hailed by many critics as a writer whose work was profoundly realistic and politically astute. Some critics believe her novel *Middlemarch* marked a turning point in English novel writing. Her other famous novels included *Silas Marner* and *The Mill on the Floss*.

As a single woman writing and publishing in an era when many women writers were limited to the genre of romance writing, Evans wanted badly to be taken seriously as a literary author. She believed her best shot at this was to publish using a man's name. Although her identity was revealed early in her writing career, "George Eliot" continued to use her pen name for the rest of her artistic life.

CHALLENGE WORDS

Word Learning—Challenge!

Study the spelling, part(s) of speech, and meaning(s) of each word. Complete each sentence by writing the word on the line. Then read the sentence.

1. **consolidate** *(v.)* to combine into one whole

    The two countries decided to _____ consolidate _____ their military resources.

2. **frugal** *(adj.)* tight with money or resources

    The Johnson family has very _____ frugal _____ spending habits.

3. **levity** *(n.)* lack of seriousness

    I was not used to such _____ levity _____ at the dinner table.

4. **pseudonym** *(n.)* a false name used by an author; also known as a pen name

    George Eliot was the _____ pseudonym _____ of Mary Ann Evans.

5. **rational** *(adj.)* 1. having reason or understanding; 2. reasonable

    I hope he can offer a _____ rational _____ explanation of his behavior.

Use Your Vocabulary—Challenge!

Film Festival The school is hosting a summer workshop for young filmmakers. The workshop has enough money to produce three films, and there will be ten students at the workshop. Use the five Challenge Words above to write a story about the students and their films.

Notable Quotes

"I am for a government rigorously **frugal** and simple, applying all the possible savings of the public revenue to the discharge of the national debt; and not for a multiplication of officers and salaries merely to make partisans."

—Thomas Jefferson (1743–1826), third president of the United States

FUN WITH WORDS

The puzzle below is only partially complete. Use the vocabulary words from this chapter to complete the puzzle, and then write a brief definition for each word next to its number.

Across

1. a movie or motion picture; a motion-picture theater
   _____

4. a plan; a scheme; something for consideration
   _____

6. tending to find fault or judge harshly
   _____

8. fear caused by some mystery or something unknown
   _____

10. to withdraw; to cancel; to take back
    _____

Down

2. a person, place, or thing that provokes thought or emotion or aids in creation
   _____

3. choice
   _____

5. a piece of sports equipment; a loud noise; an illegal business
   _____

7. difficult to understand; unable to be touched physically
   _____

9. stern, harsh, or strict with others; causing sharp pain
   _____

CHAPTER 2

WORD LIST

Read each word using the pronunciation key.

abundance (ə bun´ dəns)
blissful (blis´ fəl)
caper (kā´ pər)
cluster (klus´ tər)
deceive (di sēv´)
egotistical (ē gə tis´ ti kəl)
festivity (fe stiv´ i tē)
frequent (frē´ kwənt)
majestic (mə jes´ tik)
offhand (ôf´ hand´)
oversight (ō´ vər sīt)
prior (prī´ ər)
proclaim (prō klām´)
prosperous (pros´ pər əs)
recognition (rek əg nish´ ən)
renowned (ri nound´)
resolve (ri zolv´)
scour (skour)
significant (sig nif´ ə kənt)
virtuous (vər´ chōō əs)

WORD STUDY

Suffixes

The suffix *-tion* or *-sion* means "the act or state of."

animation (a nə mā´ shən) *(n.)* a state of liveliness; the art or work of making animated cartoons
conclusion (kn klōō´ zhən) *(n.)* the state of being concluded or ended
confirmation (kän fər mā´ shən) *(n.)* the act of making sure or confirming
contribution (kän tri byōō´ shən) *(n.)* something given or contributed
realization (re ə lə zā´ shən) *(n.)* the act of understanding or realizing
supervision (sōō pər vi´ zhən) *(n.)* the act of managing or watching over

Challenge Words

accord (ə kôrd´)
conventional (kən ven´ shən əl)
gratify (grat´ ə fī)
loiter (loi´ tər)
retentive (ri ten´ tiv)

■ **TEACHER TIP:** See page ix for suggestions on how to use this page. *Level G*

WORDS IN CONTEXT

Read each sentence below to figure out the meaning of the word in **bold**. Use reasoning skills and the remainder of the sentence to help you. Write the meaning of the word on the line.

1. At the last minute, Rachel lost her **resolve** and didn't dive off the high dive.

   strength of mind

2. A **significant** number of people gathered outside.

   meaningful or important

3. Albert Einstein earned worldwide **recognition** for his many contributions to modern physics.

   an acknowledgment of accomplishment or achievement

4. I didn't mean to offend you with my **offhand** remark; I just didn't think.

   casual or informal

5. Did you read in the paper about Terry's latest **caper** that got him in trouble?

   prank

6. Eager fans began to **cluster** around the stadium entrance hours before the concert.

   to gather in a bunch or group

7. Everyone was excited to learn that the **renowned** violinist would come here to play.

   famous

8. After the party, we had an **abundance** of leftovers.

   plentiful amount; quantity that is more than enough

9. Unwilling to **deceive** her parents, Natalie explained that she had broken the window.

   to make a person believe that something false is true; to mislead

10. The banquet staff did not serve dessert because of an **oversight**.

   mistake

WORD MEANINGS

Study the spelling, part(s) of speech, and meaning(s) of each word. Complete each sentence by writing the word on the line. Then read the sentence.

1. **abundance** *(n.)* 1. a plentiful amount; 2. a quantity that is more than enough

    We have an _____abundance_____ of volunteers for the project.

2. **blissful** *(adj.)* extremely happy or joyful

    He sat with a _____blissful_____ expression on his face.

3. **caper** *(n.)* 1. a prank; 2. a crime, such as a burglary or robbery, treated lightly

    Grandpa loves to tell the story of the great restaurant _____caper_____.

4. **cluster** *(n.)* 1. a group of similar things growing or held together; 2. a bunch; *(v.)* to gather in a bunch or group

    You must use a knife to cut the _____cluster_____ of grapes from the vine.

    After each game, the fans _____cluster_____ around the goalie, asking for her autograph.

5. **deceive** *(v.)* 1. to make a person believe that something false is true; 2. to mislead

    Don't let your eyes _____deceive_____ you; we still have a lot of work to do.

6. **egotistical** *(adv.)* 1. self-important; 2. conceited

    Denise is too _____egotistical_____ to cooperate with any of us.

7. **festivity** *(n.)* a joyous celebration, holiday, or feast

    We invited all of our relatives to join the _____festivity_____.

8. **frequent** *(adv.)* 1. often repeated; 2. at close intervals

    My parents make _____frequent_____ visits to the cemetery.

9. **majestic** *(adv.)* stately, royal, or impressive

    She had on her _____majestic_____ red robes.

10. **offhand** *(adv.)* without forethought or preparation; *(adj.)* casual or informal

    I'd say _____offhand_____ that it should cost about $10.

11. **oversight** *(n.)* 1. a mistake; 2. failure to notice something

    It was my _____oversight_____ that caused the chicken to be ruined.

12. **prior** *(adj.)* occurring earlier in time before

I'm afraid I can't come on Friday because of a _____prior_____ commitment.

13. **proclaim** *(v.)* 1. to announce; 2. to declare publicly

The judge walked to the center of the stage to _____proclaim_____ the winner of the contest.

14. **prosperous** *(adj.)* 1. having good fortune; 2. successful; wealthy

The poor family grew into _____prosperous_____ landowners.

15. **recognition** *(n.)* an acknowledgment of accomplishment or achievement

He received no _____recognition_____ for his good deed.

16. **renowned** *(adj.)* famous

After sculpting the statue, she became a _____renowned_____ artist.

17. **resolve** *(v.)* to make a decision; *(n.)* strength of mind

Did you _____resolve_____ to give up any bad habits this year?

This is a man of great _____resolve_____; he won't change his mind.

18. **scour** *(v.)* to clean or scrub

You can use this brush to _____scour_____ the pans.

19. **significant** *(adj.)* meaningful or important

My brother sold a _____significant_____ portion of his comic book collection.

20. **virtuous** *(adj.)* 1. righteous; morally sound; 2. pure or decent

He looks very _____virtuous_____, I know, but he's really a terrible liar.

Vocabulary in Action

In 1853, the Washington Territory was formed from part of the Oregon Territory. Washington, named after George Washington, was the 42nd state to join the Union in 1889. Its coastal location and Puget Sound harbors give it a leading role in trade with Alaska, Canada, and the Pacific Rim. The state has two major mountain ranges—the 7,000-foot Olympic Mountains and the **majestic** Cascade Range. Included in the range are the 14,410-foot Mount Rainier and the volcanic Mount St. Helens, which erupted in 1980. Known as the "Evergreen state," the state tree of Washington is the western hemlock, and the state flower is the western rhododendron.

Use Your Vocabulary

Choose the word from the Word List that best completes each sentence. Write the word on the line. You may use the plural form of nouns and the past tense of verbs if necessary.

On one of my __1__ trips to the museum, I spotted a guard I had never seen before. As I strolled past him, I heard him speak.

"I may not be the world's most __2__ man," he said, "but at least I'm no criminal." This was no __3__ remark. He said it with energy. I don't know what caused the guard to __4__ his innocence to a complete stranger, but I was interested.

"Why is your guilt or innocence __5__ to anyone but yourself?" I asked. I __6__ to find out what he was talking about. He told me his tale.

__7__ to taking this job, he had been the bodyguard of a(n) __8__ millionaire named Herbert Wilson. Mr. Wilson was a(n) __9__ art collector who had a very high opinion of himself. The guard described to me every detail of the __10__ Wilson mansion, more luxurious than any castle. It contained an incredible __11__ of beautiful and expensive artworks.

The guard continued, "Late one night, Mr. Wilson brought me downstairs to attend a(n) __12__ with his friends in the basement. I joined a(n) __13__ of five men and women in paint-spattered clothing, standing around a copy of a famous painting. Its original had earned the praise and __14__ of art lovers everywhere.

"Mr. Wilson asked me to help with their __15__; they were planning to steal the original painting and put this phony one in its place. They explained to me the details of their plan and asked if I noted any major __16__. They didn't want to make any mistakes.

"Did my ears __17__ me? Why would a man as __18__ as Mr. Wilson steal art when he could afford to buy it? Although I knew it would end my __19__ life on the estate, I had to stop him. I didn't care if I was forced to __20__ pots and pans for the rest of my life. I called the police. And Mr. Wilson went to jail."

1. _____ frequent
2. _____ virtuous
3. _____ offhand
4. _____ proclaim
5. _____ significant
6. _____ resolved
7. _____ Prior
8. _____ egotistical
9. _____ renowned
10. _____ majestic
11. _____ abundance
12. _____ festivity
13. _____ cluster
14. _____ recognition
15. _____ caper
16. _____ oversights
17. _____ deceive
18. _____ prosperous
19. _____ blissful
20. _____ scour

SYNONYMS

Synonyms are words that have the same or nearly the same meanings.

Part 1 Choose the word from the box that is the best synonym for each group of words. Write the word on the line.

blissful	cluster	oversight	renowned
caper	offhand	prosperous	significant

1. blunder, error, omission _____ oversight

2. crucial, vital, serious _____ significant

3. trick, stunt, antic _____ caper

4. popular, well-known, notable _____ renowned

5. flourishing, thriving, rich _____ prosperous

6. unplanned, spontaneous; careless _____ offhand

7. batch; crowd, group _____ cluster

8. delightful, joyous, ecstatic _____ blissful

Part 2 Replace the underlined word(s) with a word from the box that means the same or almost the same. Write your answer on the line.

majestic	proclaim	egotistical	deceive
abundance	resolve	festivity	

9. The queen made a <u>glorious</u> entrance. _____ majestic

10. They'll try to <u>fool</u> you into thinking there's no harm done. _____ deceive

11. Will you come to the <u>party</u> on Friday? _____ festivity

12. Thanks to a good harvest, we have a <u>great amount</u> this year.
_____ abundance

13. You don't have to <u>broadcast</u> your idea to the whole crowd. _____ proclaim

14. They worked together with great <u>determination</u>. _____ resolve

15. The character in the play is rather <u>stuck-up</u>. _____ egotistical

 **ANTONYMS**

Antonyms are words that have opposite or nearly opposite meanings.

Part 1 Choose the word from the box that is the best antonym for each group of words. Write the word on the line.

blissful	egotistical	prior
cluster	offhand	renowned

1. miserable, agonizing, depressed _____ blissful

2. unknown, forgotten _____ renowned

3. subsequent, following _____ prior

4. disperse, scatter _____ cluster

5. formal, planned _____ offhand

6. modest, humble, unselfish _____ egotistical

Part 2 Replace the underlined word with a word from the box that means the opposite or almost the opposite. Write your answer on the line.

virtuous	abundance	majestic
deceive	significant	frequent

7. If you ask him, he will probably <u>enlighten</u> you. _____ deceive

8. My window had a view over an <u>ordinary</u> wheat field. _____ majestic

9. There is a <u>shortage</u> of notebook computers at the store. _____ abundance

10. This is one of her <u>rare</u> attempts to clean the house. _____ frequent

11. I consider this a <u>meaningless</u> event. _____ significant

12. The <u>wicked</u> prince looked out across the people. _____ virtuous

WORD STUDY

Suffixes Use the words in the box to complete the following sentences.

> animation   confirmation   revelation
>
> conclusion   contribution   supervision

1. Who did the _____animation_____ for that new movie?

2. Thank you for your _____contribution_____ to the discussion.

3. Ari is an independent worker who needs little _____supervision_____.

4. Dena turned to the encyclopedia for _____confirmation_____ of the facts.

5. I was shocked by the _____revelation_____ of your secret.

6. The book came to an unhappy _____conclusion_____.

Vocabulary in Action

On March 31, 1889, a flag was hoisted to the top of Paris's new architectural marvel in celebration of the 100th anniversary of the start of the French Revolution. The Eiffel Tower is one of the best-known landmarks in the world. Construction began on the 10,000-ton, mostly metal structure in 1887 and reached its **conclusion** two years later. The tower, named after contractor Gustave Eiffel, stands 324 meters and is the tallest building in Paris. It is a wildly popular tourist destination, as more than 200 million people have visited over the past 120 years. In fact, more than two tons of paper are used for visitors' tickets each year.

The Eiffel Tower is an important part of the identity of France, so it is constantly being cleaned and maintained. In the course of a year, cleaning crews go through four tons of paper or rag wipes, 400 liters of metal cleansers, and 25,000 garbage bags. The tower also uses a great deal of electrical power, including 7.5 million kilowatt hours of energy. Eighteen transformers are used to manage the flow of this electric current.

CHALLENGE WORDS

Word Learning—Challenge!

Study the spelling, part(s) of speech, and meaning(s) of each word. Complete each sentence by writing the word on the line. Then read the sentence.

1. **accord** *(n.)* 1. agreement; 2. harmony

    Finally, the warring countries reached an _____accord_____.

2. **conventional** *(adj.)* 1. of a traditional method or design; 2. in agreement with custom

    Melanie chose not to wear a _____conventional_____ wedding dress, but a pants suit.

3. **gratify** *(v.)* 1. to give pleasure to; 2. to satisfy

    She refused to _____gratify_____ her parents' wishes.

4. **loiter** *(v.)* to hang around or remain aimlessly idle

    Kids are not allowed to _____loiter_____ outside the video store.

5. **retentive** *(adj.)* able to remember a lot of information

    I'm afraid I don't have a very _____retentive_____ memory.

Use Your Vocabulary—Challenge!

Museum Mugs A group of kids hangs out at the art museum and causes trouble. These are no ordinary roughnecks. They heckle art lovers about their taste in paintings and sculptures. Use the five Challenge Words above to write a story about these kids and why they hang out at the museum.

Notable Quotes

"The men who create power make an indispensable **contribution** to the Nation's greatness, but the men who question power make a contribution just as indispensable, especially when that questioning is disinterested, for they determine whether we use power or power uses us."

—John F. Kennedy (1917–1963), 35th president of the United States

FUN WITH WORDS

The country of Grooni has a problem. The people don't know what symbol to use for their national flag. Your job is to travel around the country and gather ideas.

The path you should take is given below. Begin your journey at Majestic, read the first clue, and determine which vocabulary word is the answer. Then head for the city with that name. Be sure to trace your path on the map. When you finish, you should have the answer to the country's problem.

Clues

1. From Majestic, travel northeast until you reach a city that is populated by "a bunch" of citizens.

2. Travel southeast to get to the town of "pranks."

3. Rest two days, then head north until you come to a town named "without much forethought."

4. Journey northeast and reach a place that makes you want "to declare yourself."

5. Hurry west to stay at the "very joyous" village.

6. Buy more supplies, then journey northwest to reach a city that is "a mistake" to visit.

7. Now head southwest to a town that "occurred earlier in time."

8. Leave quickly and travel west to get to a city that is "wealthy and successful."

9. Bearing southeast, go to a town that loves "to clean and scrub."

10. Go south from there to reach the "stately and dignified" city.

11. Grooni's national symbol is a

_____.

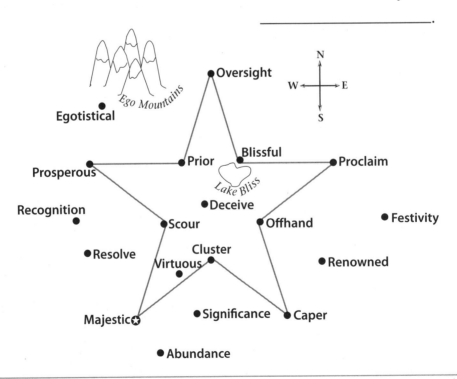

CHAPTER 3

WORD LIST

Read each word using the pronunciation key.

alternative (ôl tər´ nə tiv)
blithely (blīth´ lē)
bungle (buŋ´ gəl)
condemn (kən dem´)
contend (kən tend´)
decoy (n. dē´ koi) (v. di koi´)
establish (e stab´ lish)
indirect (in də rekt´)
irate (ī rāt´)
leeway (lē´ wā)
nebulous (neb´ yə ləs)
occurrence (ə kər´ əns)
opposition (op ə zish´ ən)
proportion (prə pôr´ shən)
provoke (prə vōk´)
ransack (ran´ sak)
reconcile (rek´ ən sīl)
resolution (rez ə lōō´ shən)
sulk (sulk)
vulgar (vul´ gər)

WORD STUDY

Homographs

A homograph is a word spelled the same as another word but having a different meaning and sometimes a different pronunciation. The following words are homographs.

bear (bâr) *(v.)* to carry or support; to give birth to; to naturally produce
bear (bâr) *(n.)* a large mammal with coarse, thick fur and a short tail

lead (lēd) *(v.)* to go before or to show the way; to guide
lead (led) *(n.)* a heavy, soft, bluish-gray metal

tear (târ) *(v.)* to pull apart or into pieces by force; to rip; to pull away by force
tear (tēr) *(n.)* a drop of salty liquid that comes from the eye

Challenge Words

amass (ə mas´)
convey (kən vā´)
hover (huv´ ər)
mediate (mē´ dē āt)
revert (ri vərt´)

■ **TEACHER TIP:** See page ix for suggestions on how to use this page.

Level G

WORDS IN CONTEXT

Read each sentence below to figure out the meaning of the word in **bold**. Use reasoning skills and the remainder of the sentence to help you. Write the meaning of the word on the line.

1. President Travis was determined to defeat any **opposition** to his plan.

    resistance

2. The burglars decided to **ransack** the apartment in search of hidden jewelry.

    to search in a disorderly way for something to steal

3. I hope we don't **bungle** this recipe, or we'll go hungry.

    to perform a task in a clumsy or an unskilled way

4. Most of us agreed that it would be foolish to **provoke** the sleeping bear.

    to make angry

5. The children skipped **blithely** through puddles on the way home.

    cheerfully

6. Before we start, we'll have to **establish** certain rules.

    to set up and keep going

7. The **irate** customer demanded a full refund and an apology.

    very angry

8. Mr. Baba allowed the students no **leeway** in choosing a topic for their paper.

    a degree of freedom to alter or vary something

9. After losing the card game, Anita ran up to her room to **sulk**.

    to be silent or distant in a sullen or an angry way

10. The lyrics to that song are so **vulgar** that I refuse to listen to them.

    coarse; crude; in poor taste

WORD MEANINGS

Word Learning

Study the spelling, part(s) of speech, and meaning(s) of each word. Complete each sentence by writing the word on the line. Then read the sentence.

1. **alternative** *(n.)* one of two or more possibilities; *(adj.)* giving or being a choice between two or more things

    We'd better go home now; we really have no _____alternative_____.

    We chose an _____alternative_____ route to walk to school.

2. **blithely** *(adj.)* 1. with little care; 2. cheerfully

    How can you just go _____blithely_____ on your way when I am so upset about this?

3. **bungle** *(v.)* to perform a task in a clumsy or an unskilled way

    Promise me you won't _____bungle_____ this job.

4. **condemn** *(v.)* 1. to express disapproval of; 2. to declare unsuitable for use

    The city may _____condemn_____ the old house on the corner.

5. **contend** *(v.)* to compete in a contest or race

    Both Christine and Becky will _____contend_____ for first place.

6. **decoy** *(n.)* 1. any means used to lead or tempt into danger; 2. lure; *(v.)* 1. to lead by trickery; 2. to entice

    A wooden _____decoy_____ floated silently on the water.

    We will _____decoy_____ the rabbit into the cage.

7. **establish** *(v.)* 1. to set up and keep going; 2. to prove; 3. to cause to be recognized and accepted

    My parents are trying to _____establish_____ a new dry-cleaning business.

8. **indirect** *(adj.)* 1. straying from a straight path; 2. roundabout

    She gave a very _____indirect_____ answer to the question.

9. **irate** *(adj.)* very angry

    I became _____irate_____ when my teacher suggested that I had cheated on the test.

10. **leeway** *(n.)* a degree of freedom to alter or vary something

    Do you have any _____leeway_____ in deciding when to move?

11. **nebulous** *(adj.)* hazy; indistinct; vague

I have this _____nebulous_____ feeling that something has gone wrong.

12. **occurrence** *(n.)* 1. something that takes place; 2. an event or a happening

A thunderstorm around here is a very unusual _____occurrence_____.

13. **opposition** *(n.)* 1. resistance; 2. a person or group that acts as an obstacle

My parents have offered great _____opposition_____ to my plan.

14. **proportion** *(n.)* 1. a relationship between parts of a whole; 2. the compared relation of things, numbers, or sizes; ratio; *(v.)* to adjust in size; to make symmetrical

Notice the size of the baby's head in _____proportion_____ to its body.

Be sure to correctly _____proportion_____ the sides of the picture frame.

15. **provoke** *(v.)* 1. to make angry; 2. to stir into action

Don't _____provoke_____ your brother with those upsetting questions.

16. **ransack** *(v.)* 1. to plunder or rummage; 2. to search in a disorderly way for something to steal

We began to _____ransack_____ the garage for a paintbrush.

17. **reconcile** *(v.)* 1. to become friendly again; 2. to bring into agreement

My mother hoped to _____reconcile_____ with her brother after the fight.

18. **resolution** *(n.)* 1. a decision; 2. an answer to a problem

The committee is searching for a quick _____resolution_____ to the problem.

19. **sulk** *(v.)* to be silent or distant in a sullen or angry way

Small children often _____sulk_____ when they don't get their way.

20. **vulgar** *(adj.)* coarse, crude, or in poor taste

She has the most _____vulgar_____ table manners.

Vocabulary in Action

The word **nebulous** first appeared around 1386 and comes from the Latin word *nebulosus*, which means "cloudy, misty, foggy." Its root is *nebula*, but the astronomical definition, "a cloud-like patch in the night sky," was not recorded until 1730. As early as 1802, some astronomers realized that nebulae were star clusters, but the distinction between gas clouds and distant galaxies was not made until about 1930.

Use Your Vocabulary

Choose the word from the Word List that best completes each sentence. Write the word on the line. You may use the plural form of nouns and the past tense of verbs if necessary.

Last semester, our school held a fundraiser. At first, we planned to hold a flea market, but some parents stood in **1** to this plan. They **2** the idea because they felt it required too much work in **3** to its relatively low profits. They suggested the **4** plan of a bake sale. The parents' committee found it a good **5** to the problem, and it agreed to **6** an annual bake sale and contest.

My mother agreed to bake several pies. On the day that she baked, we could smell the pies from upstairs. With a wide smile, my little sister Mona **7** suggested we take one of Mom's pies upstairs and eat it by ourselves.

"I don't think we should **8** mom like that," I argued. "She'll get really mad." Mona became **9** at my objection. I quickly made up my mind to try and **10** our differences. What's one pie, anyway?

Mona went into the living room to act as a(n) **11**, distracting our mom from any noise in the kitchen. I took the **12** route to the kitchen down the back stairs. I thought about my mother's delicious pies and realized that this pie would really **13** for first place in the contest. I tried to remember why I'd agreed to help Mona, but my reasons were pretty **14**. What had I been thinking? I hated to **15** Mona's plans, but I didn't want to **16** my mother's kitchen for this would-be prizewinning pie. I found Mona and brought her upstairs, without the pie.

"Listen, Mona," I explained to her. "I have always given you plenty of **17** to do as you please. But this is getting out of line. Even one **18** of thievery is too many." Mona **19** and stared silently at her shoes. I expected her to burst out with **20** language and insults, but to my surprise, she said that I was right and that she was sorry.

1. _____ opposition
2. _____ condemned
3. _____ proportion
4. _____ alternative
5. _____ resolution
6. _____ establish
7. _____ blithely
8. _____ provoke
9. _____ irate
10. _____ reconcile
11. _____ decoy
12. _____ indirect
13. _____ contend
14. _____ nebulous
15. _____ bungle
16. _____ ransack
17. _____ leeway
18. _____ occurrence
19. _____ sulked
20. _____ vulgar

SYNONYMS

Synonyms are words that have the same or nearly the same meanings.

Part 1 Choose the word from the box that is the best synonym for each group of words. Write the word on the line.

bungle	irate	nebulous	provoke
establish	leeway	proportion	sulk

1. murky, unclear, indefinite _____ nebulous

2. balance, ratio; adapt, adjust, fit _____ proportion

3. handle badly, mess up _____ bungle

4. to mope, pout _____ sulk

5. flexibility, cushion, margin _____ leeway

6. outrage, madden, arouse _____ provoke

7. institute, create, confirm, verify _____ establish

8. furious, enraged, livid _____ irate

Part 2 Replace the underlined word(s) with a word from the box that means the same or almost the same. Write your answer on the line.

ransack	condemn	vulgar	contend
decoy	indirect	blithely	

9. The invading army proceeded to <u>loot</u> the village. _____ ransack

10. Please leave your <u>ill-mannered</u> friend at home. _____ vulgar

11. You'll find a <u>winding</u> path to the playground through the woods.
   _____ indirect

12. We tried without success to <u>lure</u> the duck out into the open.
   _____ decoy

13. During the summer, my mother works <u>happily</u> in her garden for hours at a time.
   _____ blithely

14. Joe decided to <u>compete</u> for the grand prize. _____ contend _____

15. The town elders will probably <u>denounce</u> the idea. _____ condemn _____

ANTONYMS

Antonyms are words that have opposite or nearly opposite meanings.

Part 1 Choose the word from the box that is the best antonym for each group of words. Write the word on the line.

condemn	indirect	irate	opposition	reconcile

1. ally, helper, support _____ opposition _____

2. good-humored, peaceful, happy _____ irate _____

3. praise, compliment, applaud _____ condemn _____

4. straight, unswerving, direct _____ indirect _____

5. argue, fight, split up _____ reconcile _____

Part 2 Replace the underlined word with a word from the box that means the opposite or almost the opposite. Write your answer on the line.

vulgar	nebulous	bungle	blithely	provoke

6. I hope I will <u>succeed</u> at this next task. _____ bungle _____

7. That comment will certainly <u>soothe</u> him. _____ provoke _____

8. For the rest of the day, we went <u>sadly</u> about our business. _____ blithely _____

9. She has such <u>elegant</u> taste in decoration. _____ vulgar _____

10. I have a very <u>precise</u> idea of what I want to do. _____ nebulous _____

WORD STUDY

Homographs Write the correct pronunciation and definition of the boldface homograph used in each sentence.

bear	lead	tear
bear	lead	tear

1. A single **tear** rolled down his cheek.

(tēr) a drop of salty liquid that comes from the eye

2. While camping, we saw a great big brown **bear.**

(bâr) a large mammal with coarse, thick fur and a short tail

3. That tree doesn't **bear** fruit any longer.

(bâr) to naturally produce

4. Will you **lead** the way?

(lēd) to guide

5. Be careful, or you'll **tear** your jacket.

(târ) to rip

6. Some old houses still have water pipes made of **lead.**

(led) a heavy, soft, bluish-gray metal

Vocabulary in Action

The word *homonym* comes from the conjunction of the Greek prefix *homo-* (meaning "same") and suffix *-onym* (meaning "name"). Thus, it refers to two or more distinct words sharing the same name.

More particularly, a homonym is one of a group of words that shares the same spelling and pronunciation but has different meanings. An example of a homonym is *bear* (animal) and *bear* (carry).

The words *lead* (the transitive verb meaning "to guide") and *lead* (the noun referring to a type of metal) as well as the words *tear* (the noun that describes the saline substance that comes from the eyes) and *tear* (the verb that means "to break apart by force") are both considered heteronyms. They are spelled the same but have different pronunciations and meanings.

CHALLENGE WORDS

Word Learning—Challenge!

Study the spelling, part(s) of speech, and meaning(s) of each word. Complete each sentence by writing the word on the line. Then read the sentence.

1. **amass** *(v.)* to gather or come together

   We tried to _____ amass _____ enough volunteers to begin the project.

2. **convey** *(v.)* to express with words or gestures

   I can hardly _____ convey _____ my thanks and appreciation.

3. **hover** *(v.)* to hang in the air

   Dennis liked to watch the hummingbirds _____ hover _____ above the flowers.

4. **mediate** *(v.)* to intervene for the purpose of bringing about an agreement between sides

   My younger sister often has to _____ mediate _____ between my brother and me.

5. **revert** *(v.)* to return or come back

   If you leave her alone, she'll _____ revert _____ to her bad habits.

Use Your Vocabulary—Challenge!

A Bake Sale Tale Imagine that you are at a school bake sale. On a separate sheet of paper, use the five Challenge Words above to write a story about the events of the baking contest. Be sure to describe the winning food! Use the space below to jot down your ideas.

amass	convey	hover	mediate	revert

Notable Quotes

"It's the reason why I started 13 years ago on this quest, to win a championship. Along the way, I **amassed** a lot of yards, a lot of Pro Bowls, but none of that was significant because it wasn't the team goal."

—Jerome Bettis (1972–), professional football player

Secret Agent K. has just received an important message from Headquarters. Unfortunately, Agent K. has lost his decoder watch. He needs you to tell him what the message is.

Match vocabulary words with the clues below. Write one letter of the word in each blank. Use the numbered letters to decode the secret message at the bottom of the page.

1. happily   <u>B</u>   <u>L</u>   <u>I</u>   <u>T</u>   <u>H</u>   <u>E</u>   <u>L</u>   <u>Y</u>
                   1   2

2. a temptation   <u>D</u>   <u>E</u>   <u>C</u>   <u>O</u>   <u>Y</u>
                          3

3. to turn inside out   <u>R</u>   <u>A</u>   <u>N</u>   <u>S</u>   <u>A</u>   <u>C</u>   <u>K</u>
                            4   5

4. to pout   <u>S</u>   <u>U</u>   <u>L</u>   <u>K</u>
              6   7

5. to enrage   <u>P</u>   <u>R</u>   <u>O</u>   <u>V</u>   <u>O</u>   <u>K</u>   <u>E</u>
                  8

6. to declare not fit   <u>C</u>   <u>O</u>   <u>N</u>   <u>D</u>   <u>E</u>   <u>M</u>   <u>N</u>
                          9

7. room for change   <u>L</u>   <u>E</u>   <u>E</u>   <u>W</u>   <u>A</u>   <u>Y</u>
                       10

8. an option   <u>A</u>   <u>L</u>   <u>T</u>   <u>E</u>   <u>R</u>   <u>N</u>   <u>A</u>   <u>T</u>   <u>I</u>   <u>V</u>   <u>E</u>
                          11   12

9. not clear   <u>N</u>   <u>E</u>   <u>B</u>   <u>L</u>   <u>O</u>   <u>U</u>   <u>S</u>
                    13

10. to struggle   <u>C</u>   <u>O</u>   <u>N</u>   <u>T</u>   <u>E</u>   <u>N</u>   <u>D</u>
            14

The secret message to Agent K.:

<u>D</u>   <u>O</u>   <u>N</u> <u>'</u> <u>T</u>   <u>L</u>   <u>O</u>   <u>S</u>   <u>E</u>   <u>Y</u>   <u>O</u>   <u>U</u>   <u>R</u>
9   13   11   1   7   13   5   12   3   13   6   8

<u>D</u>   <u>E</u>   <u>C</u>   <u>O</u>   <u>D</u>   <u>E</u>   <u>R</u>   <u>W</u>   <u>A</u>   <u>T</u>   <u>C</u>   <u>H</u> .
9   12   14   13   9   12   8   10   4   1   14   2

Review 1–3

Word Meanings Fill in the bubble of the word that is best defined by each phrase.

1. something that solves a problem
   - a. bungle
   - b. cluster
   - **c. resolution**
   - d. jeer

2. a trick or prank
   - **a. caper**
   - b. racket
   - c. suspense
   - d. festivity

3. to scrub thoroughly
   - a. condemn
   - b. proclaim
   - c. deceive
   - **d. scour**

4. without previous thought
   - a. significant
   - **b. offhand**
   - c. imaginative
   - d. critical

5. showing great rage
   - **a. irate**
   - b. nebulous
   - c. incapable
   - d. severe

6. a place for commemorating someone
   - a. alternative
   - b. proposal
   - c. recognition
   - **d. shrine**

7. to settle a quarrel
   - **a. reconcile**
   - b. provoke
   - c. proportion
   - d. contend

8. to fake
   - a. jeer
   - b. sulk
   - **c. feign**
   - d. bungle

9. having high standards and principles
   - **a. virtuous**
   - b. modest
   - c. prosperous
   - d. egotistical

10. preceding in order or time
    - a. frequent
    - **b. prior**
    - c. preferable
    - d. blissful

11. a state of uncertainty and anxiety
    - a. inspiration
    - **b. suspense**
    - c. leeway
    - d. decoy

12. with little regard; merrily
    - a. modestly
    - **b. blithely**
    - c. indirectly
    - d. virtuously

13. an event
    - a. abundance
    - b. resolve
    - **c. occurrence**
    - d. opposition

14. a place where movies are shown
    - a. caper
    - b. shrine
    - c. option
    - **d. cinema**

15. one of several possibilities
    - a. oversight
    - b. decoy
    - **c. alternative**
    - d. cluster

16. having incredible size and shape
    - **a. colossal**
    - b. severe
    - c. abstract
    - d. prior

17. to adjust the parts of something in order to achieve balance
    - a. ransack
    - b. deceive
    - c. reassure
    - **d. proportion**

18. the remembrance of someone or something

    (a.) oversight   (b.) resolution   (c.) proposal   (d.) recognition

19. to take away

    (a.) feign   (b.) revoke   (c.) establish   (d.) provoke

20. occurring repeatedly

    (a.) indirect   (b.) majestic   (c.) frequent   (d.) renowned

Sentence Completion
Choose the word from the box that best completes each of the following sentences. Write the word in the blank.

severe	cluster	nebulous	incapable	vulgar
decoyed	abundance	options	prosperous	contend

1. I had trouble following the _____nebulous_____ plot of that story.

2. The _____prosperous_____ farmer used his money to plant another apple orchard.

3. We have a(n) _____abundance_____ of tomatoes to share with our neighbors.

4. The _____cluster_____ of carrots in the garden was eaten by rabbits.

5. The bird _____decoyed_____ the snake away from its nest by pretending its wing was broken.

6. Ruth's actions during dinner were so _____vulgar_____ that I was embarrassed.

7. Janet's excitement made her _____incapable_____ of completing a sentence.

8. We will have to _____contend_____ with the Eagles in the softball tournament.

9. Dwayne considered all his _____options_____ before making a decision.

10. Because he forgot to stretch, Sam suffered with _____severe_____ leg cramps.

Fill in the Blanks
Fill in the bubble of the pair of words that best completes each sentence.

1. Only a small _____ of the students in our class are in _____ to the dress code.

    (a.) proportion, opposition   (c.) abundance, resolution

    (b.) proposal, option   (d.) alternative, inspiration

2. My uncle, a car dealer, _____ that of the two _____, the smaller car is the better deal.
   - **a.** feigns, shrines
   - **b.** decoys, clusters
   - **c.** contends, options
   - **d.** proclaims, occurrences

3. Paula received _____ for the _____ role she played in organizing her school's recycling program.
   - **a.** cinemas, frequent
   - **b.** abundance, abstract
   - **c.** alternatives, colossal
   - **d.** recognition, significant

4. George would not _____ with me until I had apologized for the thoughtless, _____ remark I had made.
   - **a.** sulk, blissful
   - **b.** reconcile, offhand
   - **c.** provoke, severe
   - **d.** contend, majestic

5. The landlord _____ us that with the new locks in place, no thief would ever be able to _____ our apartment.
   - **a.** deceived, resolve
   - **b.** reassured, ransack
   - **c.** jeered, feign
   - **d.** revoked, decoy

6. My aunt _____ eating in front of the TV as _____ behavior.
   - **a.** bungles, nebulous
   - **b.** resolves, virtuous
   - **c.** condemns, vulgar
   - **d.** reconciles, indirect

7. Bernard is _____ about winning first prize for his _____ poem "Ode to Daisy."
   - **a.** irate, preferable
   - **b.** egotistical, prosperous
   - **c.** virtuous, prior
   - **d.** modest, lyrical

8. A strange _____ at the skating rink was my _____ for writing the story.
   - **a.** occurrence, inspiration
   - **b.** festivity, cinema
   - **c.** option, leeway
   - **d.** racket, cluster

9. Mom becomes _____ if we _____ when she says no.
   - **a.** blissful, jeer
   - **b.** irate, sulk
   - **c.** colossal, bungle
   - **d.** indirect, scour

10. The _____ cruise ship looks _____ on the sea.
    - **a.** critical, vulgar
    - **b.** severe, abstract
    - **c.** colossal, majestic
    - **d.** offhand, significant

Classifying Words

Sort the words in the box by writing each word to complete a phrase in the correct category.

abstract	blithely	bungle	colossal	contended
egotistical	feign	irate	jeered	lyrical
offhand	majestic	proclaimed	racket	reassured
reconciled	sulked	suspense	virtuous	vulgar

Words You Might Use to Talk About Manners

1. embarrassed to _____bungle_____ the introduction
2. taking back a thoughtless, _____offhand_____ remark
3. constant _____egotistical_____ bragging
4. _____blithely_____ interrupted our private conversation
5. making a(n) _____racket_____ when people are sleeping

Words You Might Use to Talk About Feelings

6. smile to _____feign_____ indifference when you are really upset
7. _____irate_____ about the snub
8. feels _____virtuous_____ when she helps other people
9. happy about being _____reconciled_____ with a lost friend
10. can't stand the _____suspense_____ of waiting for a reply

Words You Might Use Instead of Said

11. ". . . struck out," _____jeered_____ the catcher.
12. ". . . will be OK," Kathy _____reassured_____ her best friend.
13. ". . . the winner," _____proclaimed_____ the principal.
14. ". . . not fair," Anthony _____contended_____.
15. ". . . want it!" _____sulked_____ the grumpy toddler.

Words You Might Use to Talk About Art

16. a strange and _____abstract_____ modern painting
17. a(n) _____colossal_____ statue as tall as a building
18. the _____lyrical_____ poem whose words sound like a song
19. the orchestra's version of the stately and _____majestic_____ symphony
20. a loud, gaudy, and _____vulgar_____ costume

CHAPTER 4

WORD LIST

Read each word using the pronunciation key.

amateur (am´ ə tûr)

ascend (ə send´)

blurt (blərt)

critic (krit´ ik)

foyer (foi´ ər)

impersonate (im pər´ sə nāt)

incite (in cīt´)

indulge (in dulj´)

jest (jest)

mute (myo͞ot)

mystify (mis´ tə fī)

narrate (nâr´ rāt)

ordinance (ôr´ din əns)

overrate (ō vər rāt´)

pursue (pər so͞o´)

readily (red´ ə le)

ridicule (rid´ i kyo͞ol)

scornful (skôrn´ fəl)

tact (takt)

undaunted (un dôn´ tid)

WORD STUDY

Root Words

The Latin root *dict* means "to speak."

benediction (be nə dik´ shən) *(n.)* a speaking of good wishes; the asking of a blessing, especially at the end of a religious service

dictate (dik´ tāt) *(v.)* to say something aloud for the purpose of being recorded; to give orders

diction (dik´ shən) *(n.)* word choice in speaking or writing; quality of speech; enunciation

dictionary (dik´ shən ner ē) *(n.)* an alphabetically arranged book that defines the words of a language or of some special subject

edict (ē´ dikt) *(n.)* a public order or command

predict (pri dikt´) *(v.)* to foretell or say what will happen in the future

Challenge Words

ample (am´ pəl)

curt (kərt)

impart (im pärt´)

muster (mus´ tər)

rue (ro͞o)

■ **TEACHER TIP:** See page ix for suggestions on how to use this page.

WORDS IN CONTEXT

Read each sentence below to figure out the meaning of the word in **bold**. Use reasoning skills and the remainder of the sentence to help you. Write the meaning of the word on the line.

1. Let's meet in the **foyer** before the concert.

   _____ a lobby _____

2. We had a hard time teaching our dog not to **pursue** every cat on the block.

   _____ to follow or chase _____

3. Andy **readily** agreed to help us set up the tables.

   _____ willingly _____

4. She turned down the invitation with **tact** and no one's feelings were hurt.

   _____ the ability to do or say something in a way that does not offend _____

5. We have asked the author to **narrate** part of his story for our Web site.

   _____ to tell of events or experiences in speech _____

6. It is illegal to **incite** a crowd of people to commit violent acts.

   _____ to urge on; to put in motion _____

7. **Undaunted** by her fall, Marta stood up and finished the race.

   _____ not discouraged _____

8. Our teacher asked us to think carefully about the question and not **blurt** out an answer.

   _____ to say suddenly or accidentally _____

9. There are many aspects of the universe that continue to **mystify** scientists.

   _____ to confuse or perplex _____

10. The governor hopes to one day **ascend** to the presidency of the United States.

    _____ to progress or move upward _____

WORD MEANINGS

Word Learning

Study the spelling, part(s) of speech, and meaning(s) of each word. Complete each sentence by writing the word on the line. Then read the sentence.

1. **amateur** *(n.)* a person who does something as a pastime, not as a profession; *(adj.)* of or by amateurs

   Jody does not skate professionally; she is an _____amateur_____.

   I enjoy watching _____amateur_____ skating competitions.

2. **ascend** *(v.)* 1. to go or move upward; to rise; 2. to climb or ride

   We waited anxiously for the angry mob to _____ascend_____ the stairs.

3. **blurt** *(v.)* to say suddenly or accidentally

   I'll tell you the secret if you promise not to _____blurt_____ it out.

4. **critic** *(n.)* a person who judges people or things according to certain standards

   Max always reads what his favorite movie _____critic_____ has to say.

5. **foyer** *(n.)* 1. an entrance hall in a house or an apartment; 2. a lobby

   Please wait in the _____foyer_____ and Mrs. Rodriguez will be with you shortly.

6. **impersonate** *(v.)* 1. to pretend to be someone; 2. to imitate someone

   It's against the law to _____impersonate_____ a police officer.

7. **incite** *(v.)* 1. to urge on; 2. to put in motion

   She crafted her speech to _____incite_____ enthusiasm in her students.

8. **indulge** *(v.)* 1. to yield to the whims of another; 2. to pamper

   I'm afraid we are unable to _____indulge_____ your request.

9. **jest** *(n.)* something said or done for amusement or laughter; *(v.)* to act or play in an amusing way; to joke

   Alba didn't mean for you to take her comment seriously because she said it in _____jest_____.

   Are you serious? Surely you _____jest_____.

10. **mute** *(adj.)* 1. silent; 2. unable to speak; *(v.)* to muffle the sound of

    Herbert was _____mute_____ through the entire meal.

    Will you please _____mute_____ the TV while we're talking?

11. **mystify** *(v.)* to confuse or perplex

    The magician's tricks always _____ mystify _____ the audience.

12. **narrate** *(v.)* 1. to give an oral or a written account of; 2. to tell of events or experiences in speech or writing

    We need someone to _____ narrate _____ the slide presentation.

13. **ordinance** *(n.)* 1. a command or an order; 2. a public regulation

    The police have begun to enforce the new parking _____ ordinance _____.

14. **overrate** *(v.)* to consider or rate too highly

    Jack tends to _____ overrate _____ his own abilities.

15. **pursue** *(v.)* 1. to follow or chase; 2. to try to get

    Andrea has decided to _____ pursue _____ her dream of becoming a firefighter.

16. **readily** *(adj.)* 1. quickly or without delay; 2. willingly; 3. easily

    Some of the things you want are not _____ readily _____ available.

17. **ridicule** *(v.)* to make fun of

    People often _____ ridicule _____ great ideas.

18. **scornful** *(adj.)* full of dislike and critical behavior

    They make cruel and _____ scornful _____ remarks.

19. **tact** *(n.)* the ability to do or say something in a way that does not offend

    This is a delicate problem; we will have to approach it with _____ tact _____.

20. **undaunted** *(adj.)* 1. not discouraged; 2. brave

    He remained _____ undaunted _____, even after many defeats.

Vocabulary in Action

A person who acts "in **jest**" has historically been called a jester, also known as a joker, fool, or buffoon. A jester was a profession that came into popularity during the Middle Ages. In fact, a jester had a very important job. In societies in which freedom of speech was not recognized as a right, the court jester could speak frankly on controversial issues in a way in which anyone else would have been severely punished. But even the jester was not entirely immune from punishment, and he needed to exercise careful judgment in deciding how far he could go. This required him to be far from a "fool" in the modern sense. Can you think of any modern day equivalents to the court jesters of the Middle Ages?

Use Your Vocabulary

Choose the word from the Word List that best completes each sentence. Write the word on the line. You may use the plural form of nouns and the past tense of verbs if necessary.

My aunt Stella makes her living as a salesclerk during the day, but she spends her evenings working as a(n) __1__ comedian. I think that she is good enough to __2__ to the professional ranks, but she says she prefers to do it for fun and wouldn't want to __3__ comedy as a full-time career. She __4__ accepts all invitations to perform at charity benefits. She likes to help out that way.

A newspaper __5__ once reviewed Aunt Stella's act and praised her for her unique style. I thought the review was right on target. It gave her credit for her talent but didn't __6__ her skills. Even an unfavorable review leaves her __7__. She goes onstage no matter what.

Audiences love her. One night a hundred people stood in a crowded __8__ of a sold-out theater, hoping to get tickets. The fire marshal had to ask the crowd to leave; they were violating a city __9__ that only allows 20 people in the lobby.

In addition to telling jokes, Aunt Stella will sometimes __10__ a story, usually of something that happened to her. She also likes to __11__ famous people. It __12__ me how she can speak with so many different accents. She is really the queen of __13__. I've never known anyone as funny as she. But even when doing impressions of people, she does not __14__ them. In fact, she's very __15__ of comedians who use hurtful material in their routines. She believes that such material __16__ hatred.

When she's practicing, I always __17__ her requests to try out her new material on me. If I don't like a joke, I tell her with __18__ that I think it needs work. At a show, I sometimes accidentally __19__ out a punch line to a joke I've heard before. It doesn't matter, though. The audience's laughter always __20__ the sound of my voice.

1. _____ amateur _____

2. _____ ascend _____

3. _____ pursue _____

4. _____ readily _____

5. _____ critic _____

6. _____ overrate _____

7. _____ undaunted _____

8. _____ foyer _____

9. _____ ordinance _____

10. _____ narrate _____

11. _____ impersonate _____

12. _____ mystifies _____

13. _____ jest _____

14. _____ ridicule _____

15. _____ scornful _____

16. _____ incites _____

17. _____ indulge _____

18. _____ tact _____

19. _____ blurt _____

20. _____ mutes _____

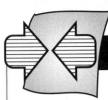

SYNONYMS

Synonyms are words that have the same or nearly the same meanings.

Part 1 Choose the word from the box that is the best synonym for each group of words. Write the word on the line.

amateur	foyer	mute	pursue
ascend	incite	ordinance	readily

1. provoke, prompt, arouse _____ incite

2. beginner, nonprofessional _____ amateur

3. entryway, corridor, waiting room _____ foyer

4. soar, scale, arise _____ ascend

5. track, seek, go after _____ pursue

6. law, decree, ruling _____ ordinance

7. swiftly, freely _____ readily

8. silent; smother, stifle _____ mute

Part 2 Replace the underlined word(s) with a word from the box that means the same or almost the same. Write your answer on the line.

undaunted	scornful	overrate	tact
indulge	narrate	ridicule	

9. He began to <u>recount</u> the day's events. _____ narrate

10. Tina fought the urge to <u>mock</u> her younger sister. _____ ridicule

11. Bert remained <u>courageous</u> in the face of great obstacles. _____ undaunted

12. My grandparents sometimes worry that my parents <u>spoil</u> me.
_____ indulge

13. Some people <u>exaggerate</u> the talents of their close friends. _____ overrate

14. I was very hurt by her <u>disdainful</u> comments. _____ scornful

15. In awkward situations, Michael always acts with <u>grace</u>. _____ tact

ANTONYMS

Antonyms are words that have opposite or nearly opposite meanings.

Part 1 Choose the word from the box that is the best antonym for each group of words. Write the word on the line.

> ascend   overrate   readily   ridicule   undaunted

1. intimidated, fearful, timid   _____undaunted_____

2. underestimate, discount, undervalue   _____overrate_____

3. descend, sink, plunge   _____ascend_____

4. slowly, hesitantly   _____readily_____

5. honor, praise   _____ridicule_____

Part 2 Replace the underlined word with a word from the box that means the opposite or almost the opposite. Write your answer on the line.

> ridicule   amateur   indulge   pursue   mute

6. The club went to see a <u>professional</u> ballet performance. _____amateur_____

7. We have chosen to <u>deny</u> your request. _____indulge_____

8. The cat will try to <u>escape</u> that dog every time he sees it. _____pursue_____

9. As the evening wore on, she became <u>talkative</u>. _____mute_____

10. The people will likely <u>praise</u> every suggestion. _____ridicule_____

Vocabulary in Action

What do the words **amateur**, *amiable*, and *enamored* have in common? They all share the Latin root *amare*, which means "to love." An amateur, in its original sense, is a person who has a love for some activity or thing. The definition of *amateur* that means a "dabbler" (as opposed to a "professional") did not become common until around 1786.

WORD STUDY

Root Words Each of the words in the box comes originally from one or more related words in Latin. Read each word history below. Choose the word from the box that matches each Latin word(s).

benediction	diction	edict
dictate	dictionary	predict

1. *prae* (before) + *dicere* (to say) = *praedicere* (to foretell) _____ predict _____

2. *e* + *dicere* (to say) = *edicere* (to decree; proclaim) _____ edict _____

3. *bene* (well) + *dicere* (to say) = *benedicere* (to commend; bless) _____ benediction _____

4. *diction* (word) + *arium* (pertaining to objects or places) = *dictionarium* (place for words) _____ dictionary _____

5. *dictio* (rhetorical delivery or delivery of speaking) _____ diction _____

6. *dictare* (to say repeatedly; prescribe) _____ dictate _____

Vocabulary in Action

The words **benediction**, *benevolence*, and *beneficent* all begin with the Latin root *bene*, which means "well." The word *benediction* first appeared in English around the year 1432. It comes from the Latin noun *benedictionem* and the verb *benedicere*, which means to "to speak well of; bless." In English, a benediction was originally a prayer said before meals.

CHALLENGE WORDS

Word Learning—Challenge!

Study the spelling, part(s) of speech, and meaning(s) of each word. Complete each sentence by writing the word on the line. Then read the sentence.

1. **ample** *(adj.)* 1. more than adequate; 2. generous

   Do you have _____ample_____ room for your feet in the back seat?

2. **curt** *(adj.)* 1. rudely short with words; 2. abrupt

   Tracy was not prepared for Marty's _____curt_____ reply.

3. **impart** *(v.)* 1. to express or communicate; 2. to give

   She has a good deal of wisdom to _____impart_____.

4. **muster** *(v.)* 1. to call up; 2. to assemble or gather

   It took all the courage he could _____muster_____ to jump from the plane.

5. **rue** *(v.)* to feel regret or sorrow about

   I _____rue_____ the day I ever set foot in this town.

Use Your Vocabulary—Challenge!

Talk of Talent It's time for the talent show! The students at your school are presenting a talent show, and you have been assigned to cover it for your school newspaper. Use the five Challenge Words above to write a newspaper article about the show.

> ### Notable Quotes
>
> "No man can be a good teacher unless he has feelings of warm affection toward his pupils and a genuine desire to **impart** to them what he believes to be of value."
>
> —Bertrand Russell (1872–1970), British philosopher

FUN WITH WORDS

Write the shortest paragraph you can using eight of the vocabulary words. Your paragraph can be silly or serious, but it must make sense. You may use any form of the words—*ascending* instead of *ascend*, or *muted* instead of *mute*, and so on.

Answers will vary.

_____

_____

_____

_____

_____

_____

_____

_____

_____

_____

_____

_____

_____

_____

_____

_____

_____

_____

WORD LIST

Read each word using the pronunciation key.

array (ə rā´)
astronomy (ə stron´ ə mē)
bewilder (bi wil´ dər)
cloak (klōk)
contemporary (kən tem´ pər âr ē)
defy (di fī´)
eccentric (ek sen´ trik)
indicate (in´ də kāt)
inscribe (in skrīb´)
linger (liŋ´ gər)
logical (loj´ i kəl)
lunar (lōō´ nər)
mimic (mim´ ik)
odyssey (od´ ə sē)
parable (pâr´ ə bəl)
quake (kwāk)
rove (rōv)
sanctify (saŋk´ tə fī)
solemn (sol´ əm)
subscribe (sub skrīb´)

WORD STUDY

Analogies

Analogies show relationships between pairs of words. Study the relationships between the pairs of words below.

high is to **low** as **fat** is to **thin**

pins are to **bowling ball** as **baseball** is to **bat**

rain is to **puddle** as **snow** is to **drift**

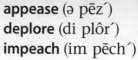

Challenge Words

appease (ə pēz´)
deplore (di plôr´)
impeach (im pēch´)
oblique (ō blēk´)
ruse (rōōz)

■ **TEACHER TIP: See page ix for suggestions on how to use this page.** *Level G*

WORDS IN CONTEXT

Read each sentence below to figure out the meaning of the word in **bold**. Use reasoning skills and the remainder of the sentence to help you. Write the meaning of the word on the line.

1. Let's take a more **logical** approach to solving this problem.

   reasonable; explainable; making sense

2. In addition to a great telescope and sky observatory, the planetarium has a number of exhibits about **astronomy**.

   the study of stars, planets, and other heavenly bodies

3. He tried to **cloak** the secret entrance, but it was discovered anyway.

   to cover up; to conceal

4. If she has a fever, it will **indicate** that she has an infection.

   to show or point out

5. The new library has an impressive **array** of books.

   a large display of people or things

6. I know you have many favorites from long ago, but which **contemporary** author do you like best?

   modern; current

7. Are you planning to **inscribe** the book that you give him?

   to write, print, or engrave letters or words on a surface

8. Mr. Collier's **eccentric** style of dress startles people who do not know him.

   out of the ordinary; not usual

9. The first space travels and **lunar** landings were spectacular historical events.

   of or having to do with the moon

10. My family likes to **linger** around the dinner table and talk.

    to delay leaving

WORD MEANINGS

Word Learning

Study the spelling, part(s) of speech, and meaning(s) of each word. Complete each sentence by writing the word on the line. Then read the sentence.

1. **array** *(n.)* 1. a large display of people or things; 2. proper order

   Jody looked hungrily at the _____array_____ of cookies in the window.

2. **astronomy** *(n.)* the study of stars, planets, and other heavenly bodies

   Ever since Ana got a telescope, she's had a great interest in _____astronomy_____.

3. **bewilder** *(v.)* to confuse or to puzzle

   I didn't mean to _____bewilder_____ you with that question.

4. **cloak** *(n.)* a long, loose outer garment; *(v.)* to cover up or to conceal

   A mysterious man appeared in a long gray _____cloak_____.

   You can't _____cloak_____ your identity for long.

5. **contemporary** *(n.)* a person who belongs to the same time period as another; *(adj.)* 1. belonging to the same period of time; 2. modern; current

   Ernest Hemingway was a _____contemporary_____ of Gertrude Stein.

   I always like to see the exhibits of _____contemporary_____ art.

6. **defy** *(v.)* 1. to stand up to; 2. to challenge

   For the first time in his life, Carlos chose to _____defy_____ his parents.

7. **eccentric** *(n.)* a person who behaves in an unusual way; *(adj.)* out of the ordinary

   My next-door neighbor is quite an _____eccentric_____.

   Isaiah has recently displayed some very _____eccentric_____ behavior.

8. **indicate** *(v.)* to show or point out

   I don't know which book to buy her; she didn't _____indicate_____ a preference.

9. **inscribe** *(v.)* to write, print, or engrave letters or words on a surface

   The committee will _____inscribe_____ each member's name on a plaque.

10. **linger** *(v.)* to delay leaving

    Let's leave as soon as the party's over; I don't want to _____linger_____.

11. **logical** *(adj.)* 1. reasonable; 2. explainable

That seems a _____ logical _____ answer to me.

12. **lunar** *(adj.)* of or having to do with the moon

Last month we had a _____ lunar _____ eclipse.

13. **mimic** *(v.)* to copy or imitate by speech, gesture, or expression; *(n.)* a person who imitates other people

In dance class, we always _____ mimic _____ Ms. Ivas's movements.

My sister is a great _____ mimic _____ and makes us laugh all the time.

14. **odyssey** *(n.)* a long, adventurous journey

Our _____ odyssey _____ began at the foot of a great tunnel.

15. **parable** *(n.)* a simple story that teaches a moral lesson

He told us a _____ parable _____ about a father and daughter.

16. **quake** *(n.)* a moment of trembling; *(v.)* to tremble

I heard a _____ quake _____ in her voice.

We saw the mouse _____ quake _____ with fear as it stood before the cat.

17. **rove** *(v.)* 1. to wander at random; 2. to roam widely

On our vocations, we decided to _____ rove _____ through the neighborhoods.

18. **sanctify** *(v.)* 1. to set apart as holy; 2. to purify or free from sin

The bishop plans to _____ sanctify _____ the shrine on the hill.

19. **solemn** *(adj.)* serious; earnest

They gave a _____ solemn _____ promise never to betray each other.

20. **subscribe** *(v.)* 1. to sign one's name; 2. to agree with something

I don't _____ subscribe _____ to that belief.

Use Your Vocabulary

Choose the word from the Word List that best completes each sentence. Write the word on the line. You may use the plural form of nouns and the past tense of verbs if necessary.

Our next-door neighbor, Kaia, is a rather __1__ woman. She wears a bright red __2__ and a(n) __3__ expression on her face. Her voice __4__ and wavers a little; the neighborhood children like to __5__ her.

She has __6__ a plaque on her door with the words "Prepare to begin a(n) __7__ of the mind." The first time we visited her, the sign __8__ me. It looked like something you might find in a(n) __9__ art museum. But she invited us in and offered us some tea. Then she began to tell us a(n) __10__ about a mouse on the moon.

Kaia seems to __11__ to the belief that one should learn something from every experience. This seems a(n) __12__ idea to me. I think she seeks these experiences. She loves to __13__ the world over, visiting friends in different countries. I admit that I sometimes __14__ at her house, hoping that she'll tell me stories and show me pictures of her travels.

One evening, we found her sitting in her front yard with a telescope, surrounded by a(n) __15__ of books. She __16__ that we should join her, and she explained that she was observing the night sky. She let us look through her telescope at the moon and showed us how to read a(n) __17__ calendar. She said that she is fascinated by __18__ and spends every clear night at her telescope. A good, long look into the sky can almost __19__ her spirit, she told us.

Kaia is one who __20__ a simple description. You might just have to meet her yourself!

1. _____ eccentric
2. _____ cloak
3. _____ solemn
4. _____ quakes
5. _____ mimic
6. _____ inscribed
7. _____ odyssey
8. _____ bewildered
9. _____ contemporary
10. _____ parable
11. _____ subscribe
12. _____ logical
13. _____ rove
14. _____ linger
15. _____ array
16. _____ indicated
17. _____ lunar
18. _____ astronomy
19. _____ sanctify
20. _____ defies

SYNONYMS

Synonyms are words that have the same or nearly the same meanings.

Part 1 Choose the word from the box that is the best synonym for each group of words. Write the word on the line.

cloak	defy	eccentric	logical
odyssey	parable	quake	rove

1. rational, sound, sensible   _____logical_____

2. journey, trip, excursion   _____odyssey_____

3. fable, tale, narrative   _____parable_____

4. bizarre, strange; character   _____eccentric_____

5. robe, cape; screen, disguise   _____cloak_____

6. tremor, quiver; shiver   _____quake_____

7. oppose, disobey   _____defy_____

8. ramble, meander, range   _____rove_____

Part 2 Replace the underlined word with a word from the box that means the same or almost the same. Write your answer on the line.

indicate	sanctify	array	linger
bewilder	solemn	contemporary	

9. That story continues to <u>mystify</u> me. _____bewilder_____

10. The records <u>show</u> his release from the hospital. _____indicate_____

11. Mrs. Torres is an <u>associate</u> of my mother's. _____contemporary_____

12. The council members spoke in <u>grave</u> tones. _____solemn_____

13. The president did not <u>support</u> the senate's decision. _____sanctify_____

14. They have quite an <u>arrangement</u> of products to sell. _____array_____

15. Please don't <u>dawdle</u> on the playground after school. _____linger_____

ANTONYMS

Antonyms are words that have opposite or nearly opposite meanings.

Part 1 Choose the word from the box that is the best antonym for each group of words. Write the word on the line.

defy	logical	linger	sanctify	solemn

1. light, lively, cheerful   solemn

2. unsound, senseless, irrational   logical

3. vanish, dash, leave   linger

4. accept, obey, comply   defy

5. curse, condemn, hex   sanctify

Part 2 Replace the underlined word(s) with a word from the box that means the opposite or almost the opposite. Write your answer on the line.

quake	eccentric	contemporary	rove	bewilder

6. Our mail carrier has a <u>regular</u> personality.   eccentric

7. The markings are like <u>ancient</u> art.   contemporary

8. Her explanations usually <u>enlighten</u> me.   bewilder

9. The house began to <u>lay still</u> after the explosion.   quake

10. It is Adriana's habit to <u>settle</u> after a while.   rove

> ### Vocabulary in Action
>
> The words *eccentric*, *concentric*, and *concentrate* all come from the Latin root *centrum*, which means "center." At its root, then, *eccentric* means "out of center." The figurative sense of the word, meaning "odd, whimsical," was first recorded in 1685. The familiar noun *eccentric*, meaning a person with such qualities, first appeared around 1832.

WORD STUDY

Analogies To complete the following analogies, decide what kind of relationship is shown by the first pair of words. Then fill in the bubble next to the other pair of words that shows the same relationship.

1. **usurp** is to **power** as
   - (a.) seek is to hunt
   - (b.) hit is to target
   - (c.) relieve is to pressure
   - (d.) wonder is to idea

2. **rash** is to **careful** as
   - (a.) best is to fine
   - (b.) clumsy is to skillful
   - (c.) thoughtful is to curious
   - (d.) little is to small

3. **irrigate** is to **crop** as
   - (a.) feed is to cattle
   - (b.) operate is to machine
   - (c.) understand is to brain
   - (d.) answer is to problem

4. **sulk** is to **dissatisfied** as
   - (a.) smile is to unhappy
   - (b.) value is to pleased
   - (c.) run is to fast
   - (d.) rest is to weary

5. **advanced** is to **primitive** as
   - (a.) prosperous is to poor
   - (b.) fleeting is to passing
   - (c.) red is to green
   - (d.) logical is to lunar

6. **undervalue** is to **overrate** as
   - (a.) twinkle is to flash
   - (b.) race is to sleep
   - (c.) deny is to indulge
   - (d.) dream is to fantasize

Notable Quotes

"Now in the sixties we were naive, like children. Everybody went back to their rooms and said, 'We didn't get a wonderful world of just flowers and peace and happy chocolate, and it won't be just pretty and beautiful all the time,' and just like babies everyone went back to their rooms and **sulked**."

—John Lennon (1940–1980), popular musician, social activist, member of The Beatles rock music group

CHALLENGE WORDS

Word Learning—Challenge!

Study the spelling, part(s) of speech, and meaning(s) of each word. Complete each sentence by writing the word on the line. Then read the sentence.

1. **appease** *(v.)* to calm or bring to a state of peace

   Midge tried to _____appease_____ Kim with a gift of flowers.

2. **deplore** *(v.)* 1. to regret or express grief over; 2. to disapprove of

   I _____deplore_____ the loss of our best teacher.

3. **impeach** *(v.)* to accuse a public official of wrongdoing during office, by bringing before the proper court

   The mayor has threatened to _____impeach_____ the sheriff.

4. **oblique** *(adj.)* 1. not straightforward; 2. indirect or obscure

   He made an _____oblique_____ reference to some past wrongdoing.

5. **ruse** *(n.)* a trick

   There was no actual robbery because it was all a _____ruse_____.

Use Your Vocabulary—Challenge!

Village Negotiations Iggy believes that other beings live on each star in Earth's solar system. Iggy has shut himself inside his cottage and refuses to come out until Mayor Mabel changes her mind and agrees to listen to his elaborate plan for communicating and visiting with the star people. Use the five Challenge Words below to write a story about how the villagers try to settle this dispute. Be creative in describing Iggy's idea.

appease	deplore	impeach	oblique	ruse

Vocabulary in Action

It's no small decision for Congress to **impeach** (accuse of a high crime or misdemeanor) the president, but in 1868 that's exactly what happened. In February, the House of Representatives voted to impeach President Andrew Johnson. His trial, with the chief justice of the Supreme Court presiding, began on March 30 with the Senate serving as the jury. Johnson was accused of having broken the law, but on May 16, 1868, the U.S. Senate failed to convict him by one vote. A second vote taken 10 days later had the same outcome: one vote short of the two-thirds majority required to convict.

FUN WITH WORDS

Read the paragraph below. The underlined words all belong in the paragraph, but they are in the wrong places. Move the words around so that they are in the right places. Cross out the incorrect word and replace it with the correct one.

It was a dark and stormy night. The moon was ~~bewildered~~ *cloaked* by thick

clouds. A sudden light shining across my yard awakened me. I watched,

completely ~~lingered~~ *bewildered*, as my ~~logical~~ *eccentric* neighbor ~~cloaked~~ *roved* from one corner of

his yard to another. He ~~roved~~ *lingered* for a moment by the gate, then moved on.

What, I wondered, is he doing? No ~~quaking~~ *logical* person would be out on a

night such as this. A sudden crash of thunder left me ~~eccentric~~ *quaking*, and I dove

back under the covers.

Now continue the story. Use three more vocabulary words in your sentences.

Answers will vary.

_____

_____

_____

_____

_____

_____

_____

_____

WORD LIST

Read each word using the pronunciation key.

approximate (adj. ə präk´ si mət)
  (v. ə präk´ si māt)

bluff (bluf)

capsize (kap´ sīz)

confiscate (kon´ fi skāt)

eddy (ed´ ē)

facile (fas´ əl)

helm (helm)

hydroplane (hī´ drō plān)

inclement (in kle´ mənt)

inflate (in flāt´)

lagoon (lə gōōn´)

obituary (ō bich´ ōō âr ē)

operate (op´ ər āt)

phobia (fō´ bē ə)

predicament (prē dik´ ə mənt)

refer (ri fər´)

squall (skwôl)

surge (sərj)

treacherous (trech´ ər əs)

unfurl (un fərl´)

WORD STUDY

Prefixes

The prefixes *co-, col-, com-, con-, cor-* are all forms of the prefix *com-*, which means "with" or "together."

coexist (kō ig zist´) *(v.)* to exist together at the same time or in the same place

colleague (kol´ ēg) *(n.)* a fellow member of the same profession

combine (kəm bīn´) *(v.)* to bring together into a whole

combust (kəm bust´) *(v.)* to burn

compelling (kəm pel´ iŋ) *(adj.)* forceful; very interesting or attractive

concoction (kən kok´ shən) *(n.)* something made by combining different ingredients; an invention

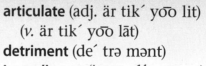

Challenge Words

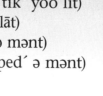

articulate (adj. är tik´ yōō lit)
  (v. är tik´ yōō lāt)

detriment (de´ trə mənt)

impediment (im ped´ ə mənt)

ornate (ôr nāt´)

simper (sim´ pər)

■ **TEACHER TIP:** See page ix for suggestions on how to use this page.

Level G

WORDS IN CONTEXT

Read each sentence below to figure out the meaning of the word in **bold**. Use reasoning skills and the remainder of the sentence to help you. Write the meaning of the word on the line.

1. You should **refer** to the dictionary for the correct spelling.

   to direct attention to some source for help or information

2. The picture shows the item's **approximate** size, but it might really be a bit smaller.

   nearly correct

3. It's time to **inflate** the balloons for the party.

   to fill with air or gas

4. Yesterday's **squall** tore a big limb from the oak tree in our front yard.

   a brief, sudden windstorm

5. With ice on the road and snow falling, the driving conditions were **treacherous**.

   dangerous

6. We went scuba diving in a **lagoon** and saw a beautiful coral reef.

   a shallow body of water, separated from the sea by sandbars or coral reefs

7. People began to **unfurl** their umbrellas as soon as the rain started to fall.

   to spread out or unfold

8. I felt a sudden **surge** of energy after lunch.

   a sudden, powerful rush or burst

9. Michelle took the **helm** and guided the boat out of the harbor.

   the steering gear of a ship

10. I wrote Lauren a letter of sympathy after I read her grandmother's **obituary**.

   a written or published notice of someone's death

WORD MEANINGS

Word Learning

Study the spelling, part(s) of speech, and meaning(s) of each word. Complete each sentence by writing the word on the line. Then read the sentence.

1. **approximate** *(adj.)* nearly correct; *(v.)* to come near to

   Do you know the _____approximate_____ number of books in the library?

   We will try to _____approximate_____ the ideal classroom.

2. **bluff** *(n.)* something said or done to mislead others with false confidence; *(v.)* to fool or mislead by showing false confidence

   He tried to fool the sheriff, but the sheriff called his _____bluff_____.

   She will probably _____bluff_____ her way through the interview.

3. **capsize** *(v.)* 1. to turn bottom side up; 2. to upset; 3. to overturn

   I'm afraid that the rough waves will _____capsize_____ the boat.

4. **confiscate** *(v.)* to take or seize private property, usually as a penalty

   The library will _____confiscate_____ your library card if you don't pay your fines.

5. **eddy** *(n.)* 1. a current of water or air moving in a motion different from the common flow, often in a circle; 2. a whirlwind or whirlpool

   The small leaf disappeared in an _____eddy_____ in the stream.

6. **facile** *(adj.)* done with little difficulty or effort; easy

   Our soccer team achieved a _____facile_____ victory last night.

7. **helm** *(n.)* 1. the steering gear of a ship; 2. a position of leadership

   The storm does not worry me if the captain is at the _____helm_____.

8. **hydroplane** *(n.)* a motorboat that skims the top of the water at high speeds; *(v.)* 1. to drive a hydroplane; 2. to lose control in a vehicle by skimming along the surface of a wet road

   Every summer we go out on the lake in my aunt's _____hydroplane_____.

   I was afraid that my car would _____hydroplane_____ on the wet roads.

9. **inclement** *(adj.)* 1. stormy; 2. harsh

   Matt hoped for _____inclement_____ weather so he wouldn't have to mow the lawn.

10. **inflate** *(v.)* 1. to fill with air or gas; 2. to expand or swell unnaturally or by force

   I think you need to _____inflate_____ your bicycle tires.

11. **lagoon** *(n.)* 1. a shallow body of water, separated from the sea by sandbars or coral reefs; 2. any small, shallow body of water

   The group went sailing on the _____lagoon_____.

12. **obituary** *(n.)* a written or published notice of someone's death

   If I hadn't read Mrs. Lang's _____obituary_____, I wouldn't have known that she died.

13. **operate** *(v.)* 1. to work effectively; 2. to perform surgery

   Do you know how to _____operate_____ heavy machinery?

14. **phobia** *(n.)* an abnormal fear of a thing or situation

   Susanna has a terrible _____phobia_____ of spiders.

15. **predicament** *(n.)* a difficult or bad situation

   How did we ever find ourselves in this _____predicament_____?

16. **refer** *(v.)* to direct attention to some source for help or information

   Let me _____refer_____ you to the librarian for help.

17. **squall** *(n.)* a brief, sudden windstorm

   The ship got lost in the _____squall_____.

18. **surge** *(n.)* 1. anything that moves in a violent, swelling manner; 2. a sudden powerful rush or burst; *(v.)* 1. to move in a swelling way; 2. to rise and fall violently

   The grass got trampled in the _____surge_____ of the crowd.

   The waves continued to _____surge_____ against the beach.

19. **treacherous** *(adj.)* 1. not trustworthy; 2. dangerous

   The hikers began the _____treacherous_____ journey down the mountain.

20. **unfurl** *(v.)* to spread out or unfold

   With pride, I watched the flag _____unfurl_____.

Use Your Vocabulary

Choose the word from the Word List that best completes each sentence. Write the word on the line. You may use the plural form of nouns and the past tense of verbs if necessary.

I have always been fascinated by old sailing ships. They seem much more exciting than today's boats, even the fast __1__. I have read many books about exploring the seas. In fact, I have an encyclopedia of sailing boats to which I often __2__.

Steering a boat today is a(n) __3__ maneuver compared to all the effort that went into getting a three-masted schooner to move. There were many sails to __4__, and a huge crew was required to __5__ all the ropes, lines, and pulleys. The captain or first mate stood at the __6__, ready to steer the ship away from danger.

Because the boats didn't have radios, crews were often surprised by __7__ weather. A sudden, fierce __8__ could prove fatal to sailors. Constant waves and strong winds could combine to __9__ even a large boat. And if the boat did not sink, waves could still __10__ over the side and wash supplies and sailors into the water. If a sailor was swept overboard, there were no plastic rafts to __11__ and use in a rescue attempt. The __12__ waters of the ocean claimed many lives. A seaman's __13__ often read "Lost at Sea."

My mom has threatened to __14__ my books. She has a real __15__ of water and worries that so many stories of shipwrecks might frighten me, but I don't find them scary. I think it would be exciting to face the challenges and __16__ of a life at sea. How would I react as the captain of a ship caught in a swiftly moving __17__ that spun the boat in dangerous circles? Would I be able to __18__ my way out of trouble if I were captured by pirates or taken hostage by an angry crew? I can imagine myself recovering from battle in the calm waters of a tropical __19__.

Of course, the stories only __20__ what it must have been like so long ago, but it's fun to read them and imagine life as a sailor.

1. _____ hydroplanes
2. _____ refer
3. _____ facile
4. _____ unfurl
5. _____ operate
6. _____ helm
7. _____ inclement
8. _____ squall
9. _____ capsize
10. _____ surge
11. _____ inflate
12. _____ treacherous
13. _____ obituary
14. _____ confiscate
15. _____ phobia
16. _____ predicaments
17. _____ eddy
18. _____ bluff
19. _____ lagoon
20. _____ approximate

SYNONYMS

Synonyms are words that have the same or nearly the same meanings.

Part 1 Choose the word from the box that is the best synonym for each group of words. Write the word on the line.

capsize	confiscate	unfurl	lagoon
squall	surge	treacherous	inclement

1. unroll, display   _unfurl_

2. disloyal, unfaithful, hazardous   _treacherous_

3. flip, invert   _capsize_

4. capture, seize, take   _confiscate_

5. severe, turbulent, rough   _inclement_

6. bay, cove, pond   _lagoon_

7. torrent, flow; rush   _surge_

8. gust, gale, tempest   _squall_

Part 2 Replace the underlined word(s) with a word from the box that means the same or almost the same. Write your answer on the line.

operate	helm	approximate	facile
phobia	predicament	bluff	

9. That does not <u>approach</u> my idea. _approximate_

10. We hit upon a <u>simple</u> solution. _facile_

11. She didn't mean it; it was a <u>trick</u>. _bluff_

12. At the <u>head</u> of our team was Mr. Lin. _helm_

13. We're in a <u>difficult situation</u>. _predicament_

14. Can you <u>handle</u> a tractor? _operate_

15. I have a terrible <u>dread</u> of open spaces. _phobia_

ANTONYMS

Antonyms are words that have opposite or nearly opposite meanings.

Part 1 Choose the word from the box that is the best antonym for each group of words. Write the word on the line.

inflate	confiscate	treacherous	approximate	facile

1. exact, precise; draw away   approximate

2. restore, return, give   confiscate

3. difficult, complex, strenuous   facile

4. flatten, collapse   inflate

5. constant, dependable, secure   treacherous

Part 2 Replace the underlined word(s) with a word from the box that means the opposite or almost the opposite. Write your answer on the line.

phobia	unfurl	helm	inclement

6. Jack sat at the <u>rear</u> of the ship. ___helm___

7. We expected <u>calm</u> weather on the day of the game. ___inclement___

8. She told me about her <u>love</u> of snakes. ___phobia___

9. It's time to <u>roll up</u> the banners. ___unfurl___

Vocabulary in Action

The etymology of the word *squall* is uncertain, but it may have come from an Old Norse word, *skvala*, meaning "to squeal." Around the world, there are many words for a squall. In Argentina, a squall is known as a *pamperos*; in Cuba, it is a *bayamo*; and in the East Indies, people call it a *brubu*.

WORD STUDY

Prefixes Each of the words in the box combines a form of the Latin prefix *co-* with another Latin word. Read each word history below. Choose the word from the box that matches each word history.

> coexist   colleague   combine   combust   compelling   concoction

1. *com + urere* (to burn) _____combust_____

2. *co + exsistere* (to appear; to emerge) _____coexist_____

3. *col + legere* (to choose; to gather) _____colleague_____

4. *com + binare* (by twos) _____combine_____

5. *con + coquere* (to boil; to cook) _____concoction_____

6. *com + pellere* (to push) _____compelling_____

Notable Quotes

"Schools of journalism at exemplary American research universities, where the academic disciplines still **coexist**, are positioned to draw upon the full intellectual and educational resources of the university environment to help produce the skilled, responsible, expert, knowledgeable and highly proficient journalism leaders that our society—indeed the world—has need of, especially in these complex and challenging times. Our democracy depends on journalism to keep its institutions challenged and responsive to the public's needs, and the quality of the profession demands the best a university can offer."

—Vartan Gregorian (1934–), academic

CHALLENGE WORDS

Word Learning—Challenge!

Study the spelling, part(s) of speech, and meaning(s) of each word. Complete each sentence by writing the word on the line. Then read the sentence.

1. **articulate** *(adj.)* expressed clearly and effectively; *(v.)* to speak distinctly and clearly

   She offered a very _____articulate_____ explanation of the events.

   I can't _____articulate_____ my ideas very well because I'm so tired.

2. **detriment** *(n.)* injury, damage, or impairment

   My father quit smoking because it was a _____detriment_____ to his health.

3. **impediment** *(n.)* a barrier, an obstacle, or an obstruction

   The police let us march in the parade without _____impediment_____.

4. **ornate** *(adj.)* very elaborate or excessive in design

   She entered the house through an _____ornate_____ doorway.

5. **simper** *(v.)* to smile in a silly, artificial manner

   The student began to _____simper_____ before the principal.

Use Your Vocabulary—Challenge!

Homecoming News The queen's ship is coming into harbor after a long journey. The town has been preparing for her arrival for weeks. Use the five Challenge Words below to write a short newspaper article that describes the magnificent welcome. Be sure to include quotes from the queen about the events of the ocean journey.

articulate	detriment	impediment	ornate	simper

Notable Quotes

"A law is something which must have a moral basis, so that there is an inner **compelling** force for every citizen to obey."

—Chaim Weizmann (1874–1952), chemist

FUN WITH WORDS

You may have heard of claustrophobia (fear of small spaces) and arachnophobia (fear of spiders). Here's your chance to make a list of new phobias people could have. Fill in the correct vocabulary word to complete each fear.

1. a fear of people taking things _____confiscate_____ aphobia

2. a fear of being fooled by others _____bluff_____ aphobia

3. a fear of unrolling things _____unfurl_____ aphobia

4. a fear of blowing things up _____inflate_____ aphobia

5. a fear of not being exact _____approximate_____ aphobia

6. a fear of overturning _____capsize_____ aphobia

7. a fear of leadership positions _____helm_____ aphobia

8. a fear of things being too easy _____facile_____ aphobia

9. a fear of water currents _____eddy_____ aphobia

10. a fear of windstorms _____squall_____ aphobia

Vocabulary in Action

The Bolinas **Lagoon** in California is a small, shallow estuary located directly along the San Andreas Fault and 15 miles northwest of the Golden Gate Bridge. This triangular lagoon is 3.5 miles long and a mile across at its widest. Like an enormous aquatic lung, the lagoon breathes in sea water on rising tides and exhales a mixture of fresh water and sea water at low tides. An average of three million cubic yards of water are exchanged between the lagoon and the ocean with each tide. The Bolinas Lagoon is an internationally significant ecological resource. Tidal estuaries are essential habitats as breeding grounds for shellfish, finfish, bottom fish, and marine organisms, and as nesting areas for herons, egrets, and other wading birds. The estuaries also provide year-round habitats for numerous endangered species.

Review 4–6

Word Meanings Fill in the bubble of the word that is best defined by each phrase.

1. to tell or write a tale
   - (a.) defy
   - **(b.) narrate**
   - (c.) inflate
   - (d.) pursue

2. one who does something for fun
   - (a.) tact
   - (b.) eddy
   - (c.) cloak
   - **(d.) amateur**

3. easily done
   - **(a.) facile**
   - (b.) scornful
   - (c.) solemn
   - (d.) undaunted

4. to engrave with words or letters
   - (a.) incite
   - (b.) sanctify
   - **(c.) inscribe**
   - (d.) mystify

5. grave and somber
   - (a.) mute
   - **(b.) solemn**
   - (c.) facile
   - (d.) treacherous

6. an extreme fear of a specific thing
   - (a.) critic
   - (b.) parable
   - **(c.) phobia**
   - (d.) hydroplane

7. to go after
   - **(a.) pursue**
   - (b.) bewilder
   - (c.) bluff
   - (d.) array

8. to let someone have his or her way
   - (a.) impersonate
   - (b.) rove
   - **(c.) indulge**
   - (d.) operate

9. a challenging circumstance
   - (a.) jest
   - (b.) lagoon
   - (c.) cloak
   - **(d.) predicament**

10. an official ruling
    - **(a.) ordinance**
    - (b.) astronomy
    - (c.) helm
    - (d.) squall

11. something that is up-to-date
    - (a.) mute
    - **(b.) contemporary**
    - (c.) scornful
    - (d.) inclement

12. to oppose boldly
    - (a.) overrate
    - **(b.) defy**
    - (c.) refer
    - (d.) surge

13. to stay for a while
    - (a.) blurt
    - (b.) indicate
    - (c.) subscribe
    - **(d.) linger**

14. not afraid
    - (a.) foyer
    - **(b.) undaunted**
    - (c.) logical
    - (d.) lunar

15. about right
    - (a.) eccentric
    - (b.) readily
    - (c.) facile
    - **(d.) approximate**

16. an enclosed area of water
    - (a.) ordinance
    - (b.) eddy
    - (c.) squall
    - **(d.) lagoon**

17. to sign up for something
    - (a.) inflate
    - **(b.) subscribe**
    - (c.) mystify
    - (d.) mimic

18. to poke fun at
   a. ridicule   **b.** quake   **c.** confiscate   **d.** pursue

19. one who judges
   a. foyer   **b.** bluff   **c.** critic   **d.** phobia

20. to take away
   a. capsize   **b.** ascend   **c.** confiscate   **d.** unfurl

Sentence Completion
Choose the word from the box that best completes each of the following sentences. Write the word in the blank.

logical	blurted	treacherous	ascend	inclement
readily	lunar	indicated	rove	operate

1. Each of you will _____ascend_____ the stage stairs to receive an award.

2. Mom's note _____indicated_____ that we should start dinner.

3. Astronauts have made _____lunar_____ landings, but no one has ever landed on Mars.

4. If I am asked to serve as president of the club, I will _____readily_____ accept.

5. Are you familiar with how to _____operate_____ this computer program?

6. After reviewing the facts, I have found a(n) _____logical_____ answer.

7. We watched herds of cattle _____rove_____ across the ranch.

8. Although it is sunny now, I am prepared for _____inclement_____ weather.

9. We read about a(n) _____treacherous_____ mountain-climbing expedition.

10. Ari _____blurted_____ out the surprise we had planned for Grandmother.

Fill in the Blanks
Fill in the bubble of the pair of words that best completes each sentence.

1. Sometimes the twins _____ each other at school, but the teachers don't think their _____ are very funny.
   a. defy, obituaries   **c.** impersonate, jests
   b. ridicule, phobias   **d.** approximate, surges

2. The _____ traveled at such a high speed that its course was not disturbed by the lake's many _____.
   a. odyssey, cloaks
   b. hydroplane, eddies
   c. helm, mimics
   d. parable, critics

3. When the famous astronaut died, the newspaper printed a(n) _____ describing his courageous _____ to outer space.
   a. critic, ordinances
   b. obituary, odyssey
   c. lagoon, eccentrics
   d. predicament, hydroplane

4. With Captain Ryder at the _____, the ship's passengers did not fear the _____ of the stormy sea.
   a. cloak, quake
   b. foyer, phobia
   c. tact, jest
   d. helm, surge

5. The duke and duchess _____ the front steps of the stately mansion and entered its enormous _____.
   a. ascended, foyer
   b. overrated, amateur
   c. roved, helm
   d. inscribed, bluff

6. The small boat may _____ if the _____ gets any worse.
   a. unfurl, lagoon
   b. capsize, squall
   c. inflate, eddy
   d. mimic, solemn

7. Because of the _____ weather, we did not _____ on the mountain peak to look at the view.
   a. scornful, incite
   b. facile, operate
   c. logical, refer
   d. inclement, linger

8. Seeing the _____ eclipse inspired me to study _____.
   a. lunar, astronomy
   b. undaunted, hydroplanes
   c. contemporary, lagoons
   d. approximate, squalls

9. My sister said the _____ taught her a meaningful lesson, but it only _____ me.
   a. ordinance, mystified
   b. eccentric, inscribed
   c. parable, bewildered
   d. cloak, confiscated

10. John knew he could _____ the odds and get himself out of the dreadful _____.
    a. pursue, ordinance
    b. bluff, lagoon
    c. inflate, bluff
    d. defy, predicament

Classifying Words

Sort the words in the box by writing each word to complete a phrase in the correct category.

approximate	amateur	astronomy	blurt	capsize
cloak	critic	eccentric	helm	hydroplane
inscribe	lagoon	logical	mimic	mute
odyssey	parable	ridicule	tact	undaunted

Words You Might Use to Talk About School

1. trying to remember not to __blurt__ out the answer

2. __inscribe__ your name on the top of each page

3. learning about constellations in __astronomy__ class

4. making an estimate of the __approximate__ length

5. think of a(n) __logical__ answer to the essay question

Words You Might Use to Talk About People

6. so shy he is __mute__ in a crowd of strangers

7. treating everyone with __tact__ and friendliness

8. unpopular because she is quick to __ridicule__ others

9. admired for being __undaunted__ by setbacks

10. a(n) __eccentric__ person with strange habits and ideas

Words You Might Use to Talk About Plays

11. a high school production with __amateur__ actors

12. a leering villain wearing a flowing, black __cloak__

13. able to __mimic__ any voice he hears

14. a script based on an ancient __parable__

15. the rave review from the newspaper's theater __critic__

Words You Might Use to Talk About Boating

16. making a(n) __odyssey__ across the ocean on a small raft

17. five-foot waves that would __capsize__ a small boat

18. the captain standing at the __helm__ of the ship

19. anchoring the sailboat in the quiet __lagoon__ for a swim

20. two water-skiers being towed behind a(n) __hydroplane__

Review 4–6   Level G

WORD LIST

Read each word using the pronunciation key.

appreciate (ə prē′ shē āt)
boundary (boun′ drē)
bramble (bram′ bəl)
dense (dens)
desolate (des′ ə lit)
employ (im ploi′)
erosion (i rō′ zhən)
expanse (ek spans′)
foliage (fō′ lē ij)
improper (im präp′ ər)
metropolitan (met rə päl′ ə tən)
nestle (nes′ əl)
pollen (pol′ ən)
reap (rēp)
rife (rīf)
rural (roŏr′ əl)
sacrifice (sak′ rə fīs)
sanctuary (saŋk′ choō âr ē)
seclude (si kloōd′)
thicket (thik′ it)

WORD STUDY

Root Words

The Latin roots *pen* and *pens* mean "to hang" or "to weigh."

depend (də pend′) *(v.)* to rely on or place trust in
impending (im pen′ diŋ) *(adj.)* about to take place; threatening
independent (in də pen′ dənt) *(adj.)* free from others; acting or thinking alone
pendant (pen′ dənt) *(n.)* a hanging ornament, such as on a necklace
pensive (pen′ siv) *(adj.)* deep in thought
suspension (sus pen′ shən) *(n.)* a stopping or canceling

Challenge Words

awry (ə rī′)
dexterous (deks′ tər əs)
imperative (im pâr′ ə tiv)
ostracize (os′ trə sīz)
sovereignty (säv′ rən tē)

■ **TEACHER TIP:** See page ix for suggestions on how to use this page.   *Level G*

WORDS IN CONTEXT

Read each sentence below to figure out the meaning of the word in **bold**. Use reasoning skills and the remainder of the sentence to help you. Write the meaning of the word on the line.

1. We **appreciate** your help with the cleanup.

   to value highly

2. The noise level in a **metropolitan** area is often very high.

   of, in, or about a major city

3. The Ohio River forms the northern **boundary** of Kentucky.

   something such as a line that indicates a limit; border

4. After Tim smelled the flowers, you could see the yellow **pollen** on his nose.

   fine fertilizing powder produced by flowers

5. Not much light filters through this **dense** fog.

   closely packed or crowded together; thick

6. The **foliage** of our big oak tree hides my tree house in the summer.

   the leaves of growing plants

7. My sister is opening a bakery that will **employ** eight people.

   to give someone a paying job

8. The land was set aside as a wildlife **sanctuary**.

   a place of refuge or protection

9. Each day the sailors looked out at the **expanse** of water and wondered if they would ever see land again.

   a large spread-out surface

10. Emma lives in a **rural** area where the mail is delivered to a mailbox almost half a mile from her house.

    of the countryside

WORD MEANINGS

Word Learning

Study the spelling, part(s) of speech, and meaning(s) of each word. Complete each sentence by writing the word on the line. Then read the sentence.

1. **appreciate** *(v.)* 1. to value highly; 2. to recognize the importance of; 3. to enjoy

   You should learn to _____appreciate_____ everything that you have.

2. **boundary** *(n.)* 1. something such as a line that indicates a limit; 2. a border

   We crossed the woods to its eastern _____boundary_____.

3. **bramble** *(n.)* a shrub with slender, drooping branches covered with little prickly thorns

   The rabbit escaped the fox by running into a raspberry _____bramble_____.

4. **dense** *(adj.)* 1. closely packed or crowded together; 2. thick

   To the north of the town lies a _____dense_____ forest.

5. **desolate** *(adj.)* deserted or lonely

   Photographs of _____desolate_____ landscapes hang on my walls.

6. **employ** *(v.)* to give someone a paying job

   Some companies _____employ_____ only a few workers.

7. **erosion** *(n.)* the process of wearing away little by little

   There's been a lot of _____erosion_____ on that land.

8. **expanse** *(n.)* a large spread-out surface

   We looked across the vast _____expanse_____ of ocean.

9. **foliage** *(n.)* the leaves of growing plants

   I saw a pair of gleaming eyes peer through the thick _____foliage_____.

10. **improper** *(adj.)* 1. not suitable for the circumstances; 2. incorrect

    He disgraced us all with his _____improper_____ conduct.

11. **metropolitan** *(adj.)* of, in, or about a major city

    There are many thriving restaurants in that _____metropolitan_____ area.

12. **nestle** *(v.)* to settle snugly and comfortably

    The two sisters like to _____nestle_____ down in the sofa.

13. pollen *(n.)* fine fertilizing powder produced by flowers

Bees carry _____pollen_____ from flower to flower.

14. reap *(v.)* 1. to cut, such as grain; 2. to harvest

We need to hire some workers to help _____reap_____ the wheat crop.

15. rife *(adj.)* 1. numerous; 2. well supplied or filled; 3. happening frequently

The swamp is _____rife_____ with mosquitoes.

16. rural *(adj.)* of the countryside

She teaches at a school in a _____rural_____ area.

17. sacrifice *(v.)* to give up something of value for the sake of something else; *(n.)* something given up in this manner

Molly chose to _____sacrifice_____ her weekend to help out with our project.

I appreciate the _____sacrifice_____ that you're making.

18. sanctuary *(n.)* 1. a place of refuge or protection; 2. a holy place

We took our binoculars to the bird _____sanctuary_____.

19. seclude *(v.)* 1. to set apart; 2. to hide from view

The woods around their home _____seclude_____ them from the rest of the town.

20. thicket *(n.)* shrubs or small trees growing closely together

The rangers began to clear away the _____thicket_____ to make room for wild grasses.

Vocabulary in Action

By the fourth century, some churches and states recognized a person's right to be free from arrest if he or she had sought refuge in a church or temple. It was from this tradition that the **sanctuary** movement arose in the United States in the early 1980s. The sanctuary movement was a religious and political movement of approximately 500 congregations in the United States that helped Central American refugees by sheltering them from Immigration and Naturalization Service authorities. The movement flourished between 1982 and 1992. Various denominations were involved, including Roman Catholics, Presbyterians, Methodists, Baptists, Jews, Unitarian Universalists, Quakers, and Mennonites. Although most of the congregations were originally located in Arizona, Texas, and California—states that border Mexico—today's sanctuary movement has supporters and advocates all over the United States and in many countries around the world.

Use Your Vocabulary

Choose the word from the Word List that best completes each sentence. Write the word on the line. You may use the plural form of nouns and the past tense of verbs if necessary.

An Air Force captain mistakenly flew his jet over the __1__ of a restricted area in a country that was at war. He found the air suddenly __2__ with missiles. One hit Captain Hamilton's jet. He ejected safely. The winds carried his parachute away from the crowded __3__ area toward the great __4__ of a wheat field at the edge of a forest.

When the captain landed, he ran into an area of thick __5__ and hid among the leaves. He managed to avoid a thorny __6__ and instead made his way deep into another __7__, which __8__ him from the view of enemy soldiers. He was glad to have landed in a(n) __9__ area, away from the nearby busy and war-torn city. He had noticed that the wheat looked ready to __10__ and hoped that the farmers wouldn't show up and discover him.

Alone and __11__, Captain Hamilton tried to stay busy by looking for food and studying his maps. He found a shelf of dirt, created by __12__, to use as a table for his maps. He felt hungry and thirsty, and his nose itched from the __13__ in the air. He nibbled on a granola bar and wondered if it would be __14__ to steal a chicken if he could find one.

__15__ fog had slowed the rescue efforts, but Marines in a helicopter found Hamilton after six days. They'd flown through enemy territory and risked their own lives to rescue him. Hamilton wept with relief and could hardly express how much he __16__ the __17__ of their own safety. In the plane, he __18__ into the warmth of a wool blanket supplied by one of the Marines. The helicopter landed on the deck of a ship far out in the ocean, and the captain knew he had found __19__. Despite his frightening ordeal, Captain Hamilton remains __20__ by the U.S. Air Force and will fly again soon.

1. _____ boundary _____
2. _____ rife _____
3. _____ metropolitan _____
4. _____ expanse _____
5. _____ foliage _____
6. _____ bramble _____
7. _____ thicket _____
8. _____ secluded _____
9. _____ rural _____
10. _____ reap _____
11. _____ desolate _____
12. _____ erosion _____
13. _____ pollen _____
14. _____ improper _____
15. _____ Dense _____
16. _____ appreciated _____
17. _____ sacrifice _____
18. _____ nestled _____
19. _____ sanctuary _____
20. _____ employed _____

SYNONYMS

Synonyms are words that have the same or nearly the same meanings.

Part 1 Choose the word from the box that is the best synonym for each group of words. Write the word on the line.

desolate	improper	metropolitan	nestle
rife	seclude	thicket	reap

1. bushes, scrub, underbrush   _thicket_

2. plentiful, widespread   _rife_

3. isolated, abandoned   _desolate_

4. pick, gather, mow   _reap_

5. urban, municipal   _metropolitan_

6. unsuited, inappropriate   _improper_

7. snuggle, burrow, cuddle   _nestle_

8. separate, conceal, cover   _seclude_

Part 2 Replace the underlined word with a word from the box that means the same or almost the same. Write your answer on the line.

rural	sanctuary	dense	erosion
expanse	boundary	employ	

9. We lived on the edge of the next state. _boundary_

10. The shop plans to hire four workers. _employ_

11. Country life suits me very well. _rural_

12. I ran into a solid cloud of gnats. _dense_

13. She sought shelter in an old shack. _sanctuary_

14. He noticed the disappearance of the soil. _erosion_

15. I love the great space of the prairie. _expanse_

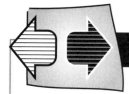

ANTONYMS

Antonyms are words that have opposite or nearly opposite meanings.

Part 1 Choose the word from the box that is the best antonym for each group of words. Write the word on the line.

reap	rife	rural	seclude

1. urban, industrial, commercial _____ rural

2. plant, sow, seed _____ reap

3. expose _____ seclude

4. few, empty, infrequent _____ rife

Part 2 Replace the underlined word with a word from the box that means the opposite or almost the opposite. Write your answer on the line.

improper	dense	metropolitan	appreciate

5. Many people <u>undervalue</u> her talents. _____ appreciate

6. A <u>thin</u> group of protesters gathered. _____ dense

7. He always says something <u>fitting</u>. _____ improper

8. People here have <u>rural</u> attitudes. _____ metropolitan

Vocabulary in Action

Did you know that in some U.S. towns and cities, the opera house used to serve as a center of community activity? Historically, opera houses have served a variety of functions in towns and cities across the country, hosting community dances, fairs, plays, and vaudeville shows as well as operas and other musical events. The most famous opera house in the country, the **Metropolitan** Opera in New York, opened on October 22, 1883. The first performance was of Charles Gounod's *Faust*, the fascinating tale of a German sorcerer who sells his soul to the devil in exchange for knowledge, power, youth, and love.

WORD STUDY

Root Words Choose the word from the box below that best completes each of the following sentences.

> depend   impending   independent
>
> pendant   pensive   suspension

1. Maggie is the most _____independent_____ thinker in our group.

2. He wore a(n) _____pensive_____ expression on his face as he looked across the lake.

3. The dark clouds overhead suggested a(n) _____impending_____ rainstorm.

4. When the storm blew in, the referees called a _____suspension_____ of the game.

5. I wore the ring as a(n) _____pendant_____ on a chain around my neck.

6. We _____depend_____ on help from volunteers.

Vocabulary in Action

Do you get a newspaper delivered to your house each day? Today many people get their news from television or computers. But for much of our history, U.S. citizens got their news from **independent** newspapers. America's first independent newspaper, the *New England Courant*, was published by Benjamin Franklin's older brother in 1721. By the start of the Revolutionary War in 1775, there were 37 independent newspapers to keep the colonists informed. During the 1780s and 1790s, citizens turned more and more to the press to keep up with political changes in the country. On September 21, 1784, the *Pennsylvania Packet* and *Daily Advertiser* became the nation's first daily newspapers.

CHALLENGE WORDS

Word Learning—Challenge!

Study the spelling, part(s) of speech, and meaning(s) of each word. Complete each sentence by writing the word on the line. Then read the sentence.

1. **awry** *(adv.)* 1. twisted or turned awkwardly; 2. away from the expected direction; 3. wrong

    Mr. Daft's plan to rob the store went _____awry_____ when the constable arrived ahead of schedule.

2. **dexterous** *(adj.)* 1. having great skillfulness; 2. clever

    With _____dexterous_____ fingers, the pianist played the complex melody.

3. **imperative** *(adj.)* necessary or unavoidable

    It is _____imperative_____ that you hand in your seventh-grade book report on time.

4. **ostracize** *(v.)* to exile or exclude someone from a group on purpose

    Some cultures _____ostracize_____ a criminal instead of imprisoning him or her.

5. **sovereignty** *(n.)* supreme or independent power, usually political

    In the Revolutionary War, the United States government claimed the _____sovereignty_____ of the 13 British colonies.

Use Your Vocabulary—Challenge!

Revolutionary Report The small country of Ilia is planning a revolution. The people want to gain independence from Oolia, a neighboring country. Use the five Challenge Words above to report on the events at the beginning of this revolution. Be creative!

FUN WITH WORDS

Use the clues to complete the puzzle. Choose from the vocabulary words in this chapter.

Across

1. The Mississippi River forms one between Tennessee and Arkansas.

4. When bees land on flowers, some of this sticks to their legs.

5. If you hide something, you _____ it.

6. A constant flow of water can cause this.

8. New York City, Chicago, and Los Angeles are _____ areas.

9. Most trees have little of this in winter.

10. Swamps are _____ with water bugs.

Down

1. A rosebush could be considered one of these.

2. Pigs, chickens, and cows usually live in this kind of area.

3. When you enjoy something, you _____ it.

7. This kind of behavior is not welcome.

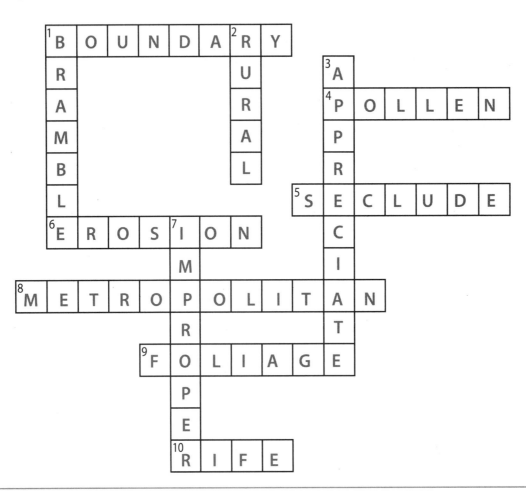

WORD LIST

Read each word using the pronunciation key.

agenda (ə jen´ də)

ambassador (am bas´ ə dər)

beckon (bek´ ən)

coffer (kôf´ ər)

contradictory (kän trə dik´ tər ē)

currency (kər´ ən sē)

grievance (grē´ vəns)

grimace (gri´ mis)

mellow (mel´ ō)

negate (ni gāt´)

opportunistic (äp ər toon is´ tic)

penury (pen´ yə rē)

prelude (prā´ lood)

premier (pri mēr´)

privilege (priv´ ə lij)

prominent (präm´ ə nənt)

radical (rad´ i kəl)

reciprocal (ri sip´ rə kəl)

republic (ri pub´ lik)

salutation (sal yoo tā´ shən)

WORD STUDY

Suffixes

The suffix *-ity* means "the state, character, or condition of."

adversity (ad vər´ sə tē) *(n.)* the condition of being opposed; great misfortune; hardship

continuity (kon tin oo´ i tē) *(n.)* the state of being continuous; an uninterrupted flow

ferocity (fə ros´ i tē) *(n.)* the state of extreme savagery and fierceness

humility (hyoo mil´ i tē) *(n.)* the state of being humble, modest, or meek

originality (ə rij ə nal´ i tē) *(n.)* the character or condition of being original or unique; the ability to act or think inventively

prosperity (pro sper´ i tē) *(n.)* the state of being prosperous or wealthy

Challenge Words

barter (bär´ tər)

divergent (di vər´ jənt)

impunity (im pyoo´ nə tē)

perceptible (pər sep´ ti bəl)

suffrage (suf´ rij)

■ **TEACHER TIP:** See page ix for suggestions on how to use this page.

WORDS IN CONTEXT

Read each sentence below to figure out the meaning of the word in **bold**. Use reasoning skills and the remainder of the sentence to help you. Write the meaning of the word on the line.

1. We mailed you the meeting's **agenda** last week.

   a list or program of things to be done or considered

2. The employees met with the manager to discuss their **grievance**.

   a complaint

3. The **opportunistic** young actor hid backstage and waited to speak with the famous director.

   taking advantage of a chance or an opening

4. Mom lets us have the **privilege** of staying up late on Saturday night.

   a special advantage or benefit

5. The move from the farm to the city made a **radical** change in our lives.

   extreme

6. She was elected president of the **republic**.

   a form of government in which citizens elect people to govern them

7. The **mellow** tones of the cello brought tears to my eyes.

   soft and rich, such as light, sound, or color

8. During the Great Depression in the 1930s, many people struggled with **penury**.

   extreme poverty

9. Helen did Jackie a favor because she wanted a **reciprocal** one.

   given in return

10. Madame Celeste keeps her jewels in a hidden **coffer**.

   a strongbox for valuables

WORD MEANINGS

Word Learning

Study the spelling, part(s) of speech, and meaning(s) of each word. Complete each sentence by writing the word on the line. Then read the sentence.

1. **agenda** *(n.)* list or program of things to be done or considered

   What do you have on today's _____**agenda**_____ ?

2. **ambassador** *(n.)* the highest ranking diplomatic official sent by one government or ruler to another

   The president has a meeting with the British _____**ambassador**_____ .

3. **beckon** *(v.)* to signal to a person by a movement of the head or hand

   I didn't see her _____**beckon**_____ to me from across the room.

4. **coffer** *(n.)* 1. a strongbox for valuables; 2. treasury or funds of an organization

   In the backroom is a _____**coffer**_____ full of money.

5. **contradictory** *(adj.)* in disagreement; inconsistent

   That newspaper article contains _____**contradictory**_____ statements.

6. **currency** *(n.)* the kind of money used by a particular country

   When she went to Mexico, Carla exchanged her U.S. _____**currency**_____ .

7. **grievance** *(n.)* 1. a complaint; 2. a cause for protest

   Chad filed an official _____**grievance**_____ to the committee.

8. **grimace** *(n.)* a facial expression showing pain, sadness, or disgust

   When I asked her how she felt about the idea, Susan made a _____**grimace**_____ .

9. **mellow** *(adj.)* 1. soft and rich, such as light, sound, or color; 2. relaxed or free of tension

   The saxophone has a nice, _____**mellow**_____ sound.

10. **negate** *(v.)* 1. to make worthless or ineffective; 2. to deny the existence of

    If he leaves town now, it will _____**negate**_____ our weekend plans.

11. **opportunistic** *(adj.)* taking advantage of a chance or an opening

    Ms. Peterson has a very _____**opportunistic**_____ approach to business.

12. **penury** *(n.)* extreme poverty

The twins grew up in _____penury_____.

13. **prelude** *(n.)* 1. anything that serves as an introduction; 2. something that leads up to

The scuffle on the playground was just a _____prelude_____ to further unpleasantness.

14. **premier** *(adj.)* first or most important; *(n.)* a prime minister

The Spring Ball is the year's _____premier_____ event.

The city held a parade for the visiting _____premier_____.

15. **privilege** *(n.)* special advantage or benefit; *(v.)* to grant a privilege

You must be 16 before you can have the _____privilege_____ of driving.

My parents did not choose to _____privilege_____ me with a higher allowance.

16. **prominent** *(adj.)* 1. obvious or easily seen; 2. sticking out from a surface or line; 3. well-known

You can recognize her by her _____prominent_____ features.

17. **radical** *(adj.)* extreme; *(n.)* one who promotes extreme change

I'd never heard such a _____radical_____ idea.

My grandparents think I'm a _____radical_____ because I have pierced ears.

18. **reciprocal** *(adj.)* 1. given in return; 2. shared by both sides; mutual

The two libraries have a _____reciprocal_____ borrowing agreement.

19. **republic** *(n.)* a form of government in which citizens elect people to govern them

Many countries have changed from being a monarchy to being a _____republic_____.

20. **salutation** *(n.)* a polite greeting

The crossing guard waved in _____salutation_____.

> ### Notable Quotes
>
> "You must give some time to your fellow men. Even if it's a little thing, do something for others—something for which you get no pay but the **privilege** of doing it."
>
> —Albert Schweitzer (1875–1965), philosopher, theologian, physician, musician

Use Your Vocabulary

Choose the word from the Word List that best completes each sentence. Write the word on the line. You may use the plural form of nouns and the past tense of verbs if necessary.

The entire island population of Deland Island excitedly witnessed the inauguration of its first woman **1** in its nation's capital last night.

Raised in extreme **2** and hardship, Sylvia Luz made the impossible rise from the barrio to the capital to become the most **3** and influential citizen of this newly democratic **4** .

The ideas expressed in her inaugural speech last night were a(n) **5** to the changes she plans for her country. It is a country whose **6** is nearly worthless and whose people cannot afford housing and food. Skeptics wonder if Ms. Luz can stick to her campaign **7** to strengthen the economy and improve living conditions.

Ms. Luz's speech began with a(n) **8** to her mother and father, whom she said instilled in her a love for her country. She then said it was a(n) **9** and an honor to speak to her public. She thanked her fellow citizens who supported her ideas with the little they could afford to contribute to her campaign **10** .

Ms. Luz thanked the former premier for his confidence in her four years ago, when he named her to be the **11** to the United States. In a(n) **12** stroke of political genius, she appointed him as her chief advisor.

Just as her moving and brave speech came to a close, opposing **13** jeered from the fringe of the crowd. Without a(n) **14** or show of impatience, she **15** their heckling by saying in a(n) **16** voice, "What is your **17** with me? Join me. Don't fight me." She **18** to the protesters to come closer and said, "Let's move toward the next century together."

Critics who hold **19** opinions from Ms. Luz's say she is a(n) **20** politician who won election by giving false hope to the downtrodden. Her supporters say she is the only one who understands the plight of this country's poor.

1. _____ premier
2. _____ penury
3. _____ prominent
4. _____ republic
5. _____ prelude
6. _____ currency
7. _____ agenda
8. _____ salutation
9. _____ privilege
10. _____ coffer
11. _____ ambassador
12. _____ reciprocal
13. _____ radicals
14. _____ grimace
15. _____ negated
16. _____ mellow
17. _____ grievance
18. _____ beckoned
19. _____ contradictory
20. _____ opportunistic

SYNONYMS

Synonyms are words that have the same or nearly the same meanings.

Part 1 Choose the word from the box that is the best synonym for each group of words. Write the word on the line.

ambassador	contradictory	currency	grimace
grievance	negate	republic	salutation

1. address, welcome _____salutation_____

2. nation, federation, commonwealth _____republic_____

3. disagreeing, contrary _____contradictory_____

4. coins, bills, bank notes _____currency_____

5. objection, charge, criticism _____grievance_____

6. cancel, repeal, deny _____negate_____

7. smirk, sneer, scowl _____grimace_____

8. representative, diplomat _____ambassador_____

Part 2 Replace the underlined word with a word from the box that means the same or almost the same. Write your answer on the line.

beckon	agenda	prelude	mellow
radical	prominent	penury	

9. If you have anything more to discuss, we'll add it to the plan.
   _____agenda_____

10. I'm waiting for her to gesture, and then I'll begin. _____beckon_____

11. I think that closing the whole school would be a drastic action.
    _____radical_____

12. There were several famous guests at the benefit. _____prominent_____

13. After a lengthy preface, Mr. Hart handed the microphone to the speaker.
    _____prelude_____

14. We spent a <u>quiet</u> afternoon playing board games. _____ *mellow*

15. I have no wish to spend my later years in <u>poverty</u>. _____ *penury*

 **ANTONYMS**

Antonyms are words that have opposite or nearly opposite meanings.

Part 1 Choose the word from the box that is the best antonym for each group of words. Write the word on the line.

negate	radical	premier	prelude

1. common, everyday, moderate; conservative _____ *radical*

2. unimportant, minor _____ *premier*

3. conclusion, ending, summary _____ *prelude*

4. support, accept, value _____ *negate*

Part 2 Replace the underlined word with a word from the box that means the opposite or almost the opposite. Write your answer on the line.

mellow	prominent	penury	contradictory

5. <u>Loud</u> music came from the speakers in the living room. _____ *mellow*

6. I've never seen such <u>luxury</u> as in the town of Falling Creek. _____ *penury*

7. Two <u>similar</u> statements appeared in today's newspaper. _____ *contradictory*

8. An <u>unknown</u> author won the prize this year. _____ *prominent*

Vocabulary in Action

You already know that a **prelude** usually serves as an introduction to a longer work. A prelude is most often associated with music or literature. For poet William Wordsworth, "The Prelude" was an epic poem he began writing when he was 28 years old and worked on for the rest of his life. Originally titled "Poem to Coleridge," the poem contained 14 "books" by the time Wordsworth died. Today many scholars consider "The Prelude" one of the most important long poems by a British Romantic poet.

WORD STUDY

Suffixes Choose the word from the box below that best completes each of the following sentences.

adversity	continuity	humility
ferocity	originality	prosperity

1. I was surprised by her _____humility_____; she hardly let me pay her a compliment.

2. After they won the lottery, the Kowalczyk family enjoyed great _____prosperity_____.

3. David won the prize for _____originality_____ in the drawing contest.

4. He continued to fight, even in the face of _____adversity_____.

5. There was a break in the _____continuity_____ of the music.

6. If you disagree with Melanie, she'll argue with _____ferocity_____.

Vocabulary in Action

Abraham Lincoln, the 16th president, was known for his honesty, compassion, fortitude, and intelligence. Some historians believe **humility** was also one of his greatest strengths. The following letter from Lincoln to Lydia Bixbie, who lost five sons in the Civil War, shows his humility:

Executive Mansion
Washington, Nov. 21, 1864

Dear Madam,

I have been shown in the files of the War Department a statement of the Adjutant General of Massachusetts that you are the mother of five sons who have died gloriously on the field of battle. I feel how weak and fruitless must be any word of mine which should attempt to beguile you from the grief of a loss so overwhelming. But I cannot refrain from tendering you the consolation that may be found in the thanks of the republic they died to save. I pray that our Heavenly Father may assuage the anguish of your bereavement, and leave you only the cherished memory of the loved and lost, and the solemn pride that must be yours to have laid so costly a sacrifice upon the altar of freedom.

Yours very sincerely and respectfully,

A. Lincoln

CHALLENGE WORDS

Word Learning—Challenge!

Study the spelling, part(s) of speech, and meaning(s) of each word. Complete each sentence by writing the word on the line. Then read the sentence.

1. **barter** *(v.)* to trade one item or service for another

   Most human beings used to _____barter_____ before they had money.

2. **divergent** *(adj.)* 1. differing or varying; 2. going off in different directions

   They have _____divergent_____ ideas on the matter.

3. **impunity** *(n.)* freedom from punishment

   The queen's brother robbed the villagers with _____impunity_____.

4. **perceptible** *(adj.)* 1. capable of being recognized by the senses; 2. apparent

   The smell of burning cake was barely _____perceptible_____.

5. **suffrage** *(n.)* 1. the right to vote; 2. the act of casting a vote

   In the United States, _____suffrage_____ was granted to African American men in 1870 and to all women in 1920.

Use Your Vocabulary—Challenge!

Presidential Debate The two presidential candidates are meeting for a debate. One of them wants to radically change the way the country works. Use the five Challenge Words above to write a script for this debate. Use your imagination!

> ## Notable Quotes
>
> "If we had no winter, the spring would not be so pleasant: if we did not sometimes taste of **adversity**, prosperity would not be so welcome."
>
> —Anne Bradstreet (1612–1672), poet
> (from *Meditations Divine and Moral*, 1655)

Eleven vocabulary words from this chapter are hidden in the following list of addresses. Underline the words. Then use five of the words in sentences.

A. M. Bassadory
12 East Twelfth St.
Frepubli City, TN

Mell Owens
Prominent Station #43
Cagenday, Arizona

Sal Utationi
1900 Coffer Rd.
Nebarker, NJ

Pen Uryllis
900 N. Ega Terrace
Olulu, HI

P. R. Emier
1053 Elm Street
Radi, California

Answers will vary, but should include five of the following words: ambassador, republic, mellow, prominent, agenda, salutation, coffer, penury, negate, premier, radical.

1. _____

_____

2. _____

_____

3. _____

_____

4. _____

_____

5. _____

_____

WORD LIST

Read each word using the pronunciation key.

bicker (bik´ ər)
blunder (blun´ dər)
bountiful (boun´ tə fəl)
coincidence (kō in´ sə dəns)
designate (dez´ ig nāt)
devour (di vour´)
extol (ek stōl´)
gravely (grāv´ lē)
impostor (im päs´ tər)
lure (lo͞or)
meddlesome (med´ əl səm)
nudge (nuj)
primitive (prim´ ə tiv)
prolong (prə lôŋ´)
rampage (ram´ pāj)
repel (ri pel´)
repent (ri pent´)
righteous (rī´ chəs)
rival (rī´ vəl)
thrive (thrīv)

WORD STUDY

Analogies

Analogies show relationships between pairs of words. Study the relationships between the pairs of words below.

ink is to **pen** as **paint** is to **brush**

laugh is to **funny** as **weep** is to **sad**

dirt is to **brown** as **sky** is to **blue**

Challenge Words

bibliography (bib lē og´ rə fē)
emancipation (i man sə pā´ shən)
expedite (ek´ spə dīt)
incipient (in sip´ ē ənt)
personify (pər son´ ə fī)

■ **TEACHER TIP:** See page ix for suggestions on how to use this page.

WORDS IN CONTEXT

Read each sentence below to figure out the meaning of the word in **bold**. Use reasoning skills and the remainder of the sentence to help you. Write the meaning of the word on the line.

1. On Friday night, the football team will play our crosstown **rivals**, the Lions.

    those who compete with another

2. Plants **thrive** in good soil with plenty of sunshine and water.

    to do well in one's surroundings

3. Janet promised to **nudge** me each time I sing off-key at choir rehearsal.

    to give a gentle push to

4. Don't **prolong** our suspense; tell us if you won the award!

    to lengthen in time

5. The starving peasants went on a **rampage** and stormed the castle walls.

    violent action or behavior

6. My brother and I used to **bicker** all the time, but now he is my best friend.

    to quarrel about something unimportant; to squabble

7. We had a **bountiful** harvest this year and celebrated with a party for the neighbors.

    more than enough; plentiful

8. It is a **coincidence** that I have two teachers named Ms. Beaker.

    the chance occurrence of two things at the same time or place

9. **Designate** your choice by marking the correct box.

    to point out or indicate

10. I made a **blunder** and left the party in someone else's coat.

    a stupid mistake

WORD MEANINGS

Word Learning

Study the spelling, part(s) of speech, and meaning(s) of each word. Complete each sentence by writing the word on the line. Then read the sentence.

1. **bicker** *(v.)* 1. to quarrel about something unimportant; 2. to squabble

    My mother warned us not to _____ bicker _____ while she was gone.

2. **blunder** *(n.)* a stupid mistake; *(v.)* 1. to make a stupid mistake; 2. to move clumsily or stumble

    That was an awful _____ blunder _____ if I ever saw one.

    Sean opened the door to see Uncle Joe _____ blunder _____ into the room.

3. **bountiful** *(adj.)* more than enough; plentiful

    The people prepared a _____ bountiful _____ feast.

4. **coincidence** *(n.)* the chance occurrence of two things at the same time or place

    It was a strange _____ coincidence _____ that we should meet at the park.

5. **designate** *(v.)* 1. to point out or indicate; 2. to name

    Now you have to _____ designate _____ a team captain.

6. **devour** *(v.)* 1. to eat hungrily or greedily; 2. to consume

    She can _____ devour _____ that plate of food in a minute.

7. **extol** *(v.)* to praise lavishly

    My teachers always _____ extol _____ the virtues of hard work.

8. **gravely** *(adv.)* 1. seriously; 2. importantly

    The nurse is _____ gravely _____ concerned about your health.

9. **impostor** *(n.)* someone who is pretending to be another, in order to deceive

    That's not Santa Claus! It's an _____ impostor _____ .

10. **lure** *(n.)* something that entices or attracts with the promise of a reward; *(v.)* to attract, entice, or tempt

    She tied a fishing _____ lure _____ to the end of her line.

    Try to _____ lure _____ the animals in here with food.

11. **meddlesome** *(adj.)* inclined to intrude in other people's affairs

I was told by a _____meddlesome_____ acquaintance that my two brothers had a fight.

12. **nudge** *(v.)* to give a gentle push to; *(n.)* a gentle push

She tried to _____nudge_____ her sister toward the door.

Pete gave me a little _____nudge_____ in the arm.

13. **primitive** *(adj.)* 1. early or first; 2. simple; *(n.)* a primitive person or thing

Did you see the photos of _____primitive_____ cave drawings?

He considers me a _____primitive_____ just because I walk to school.

14. **prolong** *(v.)* to lengthen in time

I'd love to _____prolong_____ our visit, but we have to go home.

15. **rampage** *(n.)* violent action or behavior; *(v.)* to move about violently

You'd better look out when Marty's on a _____rampage_____.

From our jeep in the desert, we could watch the lions _____rampage_____.

16. **repel** *(v.)* 1. to drive back; 2. to cause disgust in; 3. to push away

The army managed to _____repel_____ the attackers.

17. **repent** *(v.)* 1. to feel sorry; 2. to make up for past mistakes

I will _____repent_____ for the thoughtless comments I made.

18. **righteous** *(adj.)* doing what is right and moral

Chris is a good and _____righteous_____ person.

19. **rival** *(n.)* one who competes with another

That's my tennis _____rival_____ over there.

20. **thrive** *(v.)* to do well in one's surroundings

Alligators _____thrive_____ in the swamps.

Notable Quotes

"The company of just and **righteous** men is better than wealth and a rich estate."

—Euripides, (484–406 BC), Greek playwright (from *Aegeus*)

Use Your Vocabulary

Choose the word from the Word List that best completes each sentence. Write the word on the line. You may use the plural form of nouns and the past tense of verbs if necessary.

Our family had such a good time visiting Texas that we decided to __1__ our vacation. Dad phoned our __2__ neighbor to let her know when we would be home. He was afraid that she would report us missing otherwise.

Texas has many __3__ . For one thing, we love to watch basketball. I like the San Antonio Spurs, and my brother likes their __4__ , the Houston Rockets. We began to argue over which team to see, but my mother __5__ my arm and pointed to the newspaper.

"Don't __6__ ," she said. "Look at this. The Spurs are playing the Rockets in San Antonio tomorrow night. What a(n) __7__ !" My brother and I __8__ immediately for quarreling, and my father began to __9__ the virtues of San Antonio and its __10__ sights and activities. He drew us a(n) __11__ map of the city and told us to __12__ the things we would like to see.

I took one look at his scratchy drawing of the city's layout. "Dad," I said __13__ . "We can't tell anything from this map. I think we need to just go there and see what we find." He apologized for the __14__ and agreed that we should just hit the road.

Once we got to San Antonio, we __15__ a meal at a great Mexican restaurant. Then we proceeded to the Alamo, where we learned about the Texans' attempts to __16__ the attacking Mexican army. At the zoo, our tour guide explained that the animals __17__ because they are kept in large, open spaces instead of small cages. She said that the big cats need room to __18__ as they would in the wild.

At the end of the day, my parents praised us for behaving in such a(n) __19__ manner. My mother said that we had behaved so well that we might have been a couple of __20__ instead of her real children!

1. _____ prolong _____
2. _____ meddlesome _____
3. _____ lures _____
4. _____ rivals _____
5. _____ nudged _____
6. _____ bicker _____
7. _____ coincidence _____
8. _____ repented _____
9. _____ extol _____
10. _____ bountiful _____
11. _____ primitive _____
12. _____ designate _____
13. _____ gravely _____
14. _____ blunder _____
15. _____ devoured _____
16. _____ repel _____
17. _____ thrive _____
18. _____ rampage _____
19. _____ righteous _____
20. _____ impostors _____

SYNONYMS

Synonyms are words that have the same or nearly the same meanings.

Part 1 Choose the word from the box that is the best synonym for each group of words. Write the word on the line.

bicker	rival	extol	impostor
lure	rampage	righteous	bountiful

1. argue, wrangle   _____bicker_____

2. attraction; coax, bait   _____lure_____

3. upright, good, just   _____righteous_____

4. acclaim, applaud, glorify   _____extol_____

5. lavish, generous, vast   _____bountiful_____

6. uproar, tantrum   _____rampage_____

7. pretender, fraud, cheat   _____impostor_____

8. opponent, competitor, contestant   _____rival_____

Part 2 Replace the underlined word(s) with a word from the box that means the same or almost the same. Write your answer on the line.

thrive	repel	devour	blunder
repent	meddlesome	designate	

9. The weeds seem to <u>flourish</u> in my garden. _____thrive_____

10. I'm sorry about the <u>slip-up</u>; it won't happen again. _____blunder_____

11. We have yet to <u>appoint</u> a leader. _____designate_____

12. I hope we'll be able to <u>ward off</u> any attacks. _____repel_____

13. I think that she will come to <u>regret</u> what she's done. _____repent_____

14. Don't just <u>wolf down</u> the whole meal as soon as it arrives. _____devour_____

15. Let's have this conversation away from <u>prying</u> eyes and ears.
_____meddlesome_____

ANTONYMS

Antonyms are words that have opposite or nearly opposite meanings.

Part 1 Choose the word from the box that is the best antonym for each group of words. Write the word on the line.

bountiful	lure	primitive	repel	righteous

1. discouragement; repel, deter   _____lure_____

2. insufficient, rare, scarce   _____bountiful_____

3. draw near, attract   _____repel_____

4. immoral, unjust, evil   _____righteous_____

5. sophisticated, polished, modern   _____primitive_____

Part 2 Replace the underlined word with a word from the box that means the opposite or almost the opposite. Write your answer on the line.

extol	thrive	gravely	prolong	rival

6. The committee <u>gaily</u> discussed plans for the future. _____gravely_____

7. I think they will <u>condemn</u> the works of the mayor. _____extol_____

8. We tried to <u>shorten</u> the conversation with him. _____prolong_____

9. Come and meet Lilly, my debate <u>partner</u>. _____rival_____

10. The deer population will <u>decline</u> in the forest preserve. _____thrive_____

Vocabulary in Action

It was 1804. Alexander Hamilton, former secretary of the treasury, and Vice President Aaron Burr were longstanding political **rivals** and personal enemies. Burr might have been the president had it not been for Hamilton's interference. When Burr's term as vice president was almost over, he ran for governor of New York. Hamilton, once again, prevented Burr from winning by opposing his candidacy. Burr retaliated by challenging Hamilton to a duel. Standing on the heights of Weehawken, New Jersey on the morning of July 11, Hamilton and Burr fired their pistols. Some people said that Hamilton purposely missed Burr. Burr's shot, however, fatally wounded Hamilton, leading to his death the next day. Burr walked away unharmed.

WORD STUDY

Analogies To complete the following analogies, decide what kind of relationship is shown by the first pair of words. Then fill in the bubble next to the other pair of words that show the same relationship.

1. **curious** is to **knowledge** as
   - a. ridiculous is to joke
   - b. angry is to punishment
   - c. hungry is to food
   - d. wonderful is to idea

2. **weapon** is to **fight** as
   - a. gun is to bullet
   - b. paint is to brush
   - c. food is to eat
   - d. pen is to write

3. **syrup** is to **maple tree** as
   - a. butter is to cow
   - b. syrup is to pancakes
   - c. leaf is to bush
   - d. mower is to grass

4. **lawyer** is to **logic** as
   - a. doctor is to hospital
   - b. police officer is to criminal
   - c. student is to homework
   - d. artist is to creativity

5. **ballad** is to **song** as
   - a. cousin is to relative
   - b. house is to mansion
   - c. rake is to garden
   - d. weed is to flower

6. **thaw** is to **spring** as
   - a. melt is to summer
   - b. slip is to winter
   - c. freeze is to winter
   - d. sweat is to summer

CHALLENGE WORDS

Word Learning—Challenge!

Study the spelling, part(s) of speech, and meaning(s) of each word. Complete each sentence by writing the word on the line. Then read the sentence.

1. **bibliography** *(n.)* 1. a list of books about a particular topic; 2. a list of resources used in the preparation of a work

   I have only three books listed in my ____bibliography____.

2. **emancipation** *(n.)* the act of freeing

   The _____ of African American slaves occurred in 1861.
   emancipation

3. **expedite** *(v.)* to speed up the process or progress of

   If you carry fewer provisions, you will _____ your climb up the mountain.
   expedite

4. **incipient** *(adj.)* beginning to exist or become apparent

   Fortunately, doctors caught the disease at an _____ stage.
   incipient

5. **personify** *(v.)* 1. to represent a nonhuman thing as having human powers or characteristics; 2. to typify or embody

   Our delightful new editor will _____ the charming feel of this magazine.
   personify

Use Your Vocabulary—Challenge!

Finding Freedom Fighters Calvin has to write a report about a person who has fought for freedom in some way. He's having a hard time deciding who and what to write about. Use the five Challenge Words below to write a story about what Calvin discovers at the library.

bibliography	emancipation	expedite	incipient	personify

FUN WITH WORDS

Let's take a trip to Texas. Below is a list of places to visit and a brief statement about each one. Beside each statement is a vocabulary word from this chapter. Write a sentence about the place, using the vocabulary word. The first one is done for you.

1. Seminole Canyon State Historical Park—rock art in caves; primitive

   We hiked into a cave at Seminole Canyon State Historical Park and saw primitive art

   on the walls.

2. McDonald Observatory—night events for stargazers; bountiful

   Answers will vary.

3. Port Aransas—camping on the beach; extol

_____

_____

4. Lake Somerville—trails for horseback riding; nudge

_____

_____

5. Caddo Lake—fishing and boating; lure

_____

_____

6. Davis Mountains—a 75-mile scenic loop; prolong

_____

_____

7. Casa Navarro State Historical Park—restored home of a pioneer; gravely

_____

_____

8. Aransas National Wildlife Refuge—home of whooping cranes in winter; thrive

_____

_____

9. Lyndon B. Johnson National Historical Park—home of former president; designate

_____

_____

10. Minute Maid Park—home of Houston Astros baseball team; rival

_____

_____

Review 7–9

Word Meanings Fill in the bubble of the word that is best defined by each phrase.

1. relating to a major city
   - (a.) rural
   - **(b.) metropolitan**
   - (c.) prominent
   - (d.) meddlesome

2. a place that provides protection
   - (a.) republic
   - (b.) pollen
   - **(c.) sanctuary**
   - (d.) rival

3. the money of a certain country
   - (a.) coffer
   - (b.) thicket
   - (c.) grievance
   - **(d.) currency**

4. to move clumsily or thoughtlessly
   - (a.) lure
   - **(b.) blunder**
   - (c.) sacrifice
   - (d.) reap

5. a greeting to another person
   - (a.) ambassador
   - **(b.) salutation**
   - (c.) grievance
   - (d.) boundary

6. to make last longer
   - (a.) thrive
   - (b.) repent
   - **(c.) prolong**
   - (d.) nestle

7. a large, unbroken space
   - **(a.) expanse**
   - (b.) foliage
   - (c.) thicket
   - (d.) sanctuary

8. a person who wants great changes
   - (a.) premier
   - (b.) rampage
   - (c.) impostor
   - **(d.) radical**

9. the process of being worn away
   - **(a.) erosion**
   - (b.) bramble
   - (c.) nudge
   - (d.) salutation

10. to eat in a greedy way
    - (a.) negate
    - (b.) employ
    - (c.) reap
    - **(d.) devour**

11. a competitor
    - (a.) radical
    - (b.) lure
    - **(c.) rival**
    - (d.) penury

12. to give up something precious
    - (a.) seclude
    - **(b.) sacrifice**
    - (c.) extol
    - (d.) prolong

13. an introductory part
    - (a.) privilege
    - **(b.) prelude**
    - (c.) currency
    - (d.) agenda

14. empty; without hope
    - (a.) bountiful
    - (b.) primitive
    - **(c.) desolate**
    - (d.) opportunistic

15. to choose or appoint
    - (a.) appreciate
    - (b.) rampage
    - **(c.) designate**
    - (d.) bicker

16. to turn or keep away
    - (a.) devour
    - (b.) blunder
    - (c.) employ
    - **(d.) repel**

17. expressing an opposite idea
    - **(a.) contradictory**
    - (b.) dense
    - (c.) righteous
    - (d.) improper

18. common or widespread

    (**a.**)reciprocal   (**b.**)mellow   (**c.**)rife   (**d.**)desolate

19. a nation with elected officials

    (**a.**)coffer   (**b.**)republic   (**c.**)boundary   (**d.**)penury

20. a list of things to be done at a meeting

    (**a.**)privilege   (**b.**)coincidence   (**c.**)premier   (**d.**)agenda

Sentence Completion Choose the word from the box that best completes each of the following sentences. Write the word in the blank.

gravely	ambassador	pollen	grimace	reciprocal
appreciate	improper	extolled	thrive	brambles

1. We ___appreciate___ all your hard work setting up the school carnival.

2. I wore gloves so I wouldn't get scratched by the ___brambles___ when we were picking berries.

3. The president asked the French ___ambassador___ to join the meeting.

4. The ___grimace___ on Martin's face showed he was not ready for a quiz.

5. The movie critic ___extolled___ the young actor's performance.

6. Babies ___thrive___ when they are fed well and given plenty of affection.

7. It is ___improper___ for you to wear your hat at the dinner table.

8. When I smelled the flower, I got ___pollen___ on my nose.

9. I am ___gravely___ concerned about the drop in your grade point average.

10. My friend and I made a(n) ___reciprocal___ agreement that he makes me cookies and I wash his car.

Fill in the Blanks Fill in the bubble of the pair of words that best completes each sentence.

1. Since we live in a _____ apartment, we will spend our vacation in a _____ cabin.

    (**a.**) dense, radical   (**c.**)metropolitan, rural

    (**b.**) meddlesome, primitive   (**d.**)righteous, bountiful

2. Each time the two sisters _____, their father took away one of their _____.

   a. appreciated, preludes   **c.** rampaged, blunders

   b. bickered, privileges   **d.** nudged, agendas

3. Each night, the salesclerk places all the American _____ in a special _____.

   a. penury, pollen   **c.** republic, salutation

   b. foliage, thicket   **d.** currency, coffer

4. The bear went on a _____ and destroyed the _____.

   a. rampage, thicket   **c.** blunder, sanctuary

   b. grievance, impostor   **d.** grimace, agenda

5. The _____ negotiated a _____ trade agreement between the two countries.

   a. coincidence, primitive   **c.** ambassador, reciprocal

   b. prelude, prominent   **d.** rival, mellow

6. During the thunderstorm, the hikers found _____ in the _____ hut.

   a. penury, bountiful   **c.** sacrifice, mellow

   b. agenda, desolate   **d.** sanctuary, primitive

7. We discovered he was a(n) _____ when he gave _____ answers to our questions.

   a. ambassador, premier   **c.** expanse, meddlesome

   b. impostor, contradictory   **d.** rival, dense

8. The surgeon _____ a(n) _____ new technique to save her patient's life.

   a. employed, radical   **c.** negated, mellow

   b. repented, righteous   **d.** nestled, improper

9. It was no _____ that our _____ neighbor happened to be standing where he could hear us.

   a. penury, opportunistic   **c.** coincidence, meddlesome

   b. currency, premier   **d.** erosion, contradictory

10. Koalas _____ on the _____ of eucalyptus trees.

   a. thrive, foliage   **c.** beckon, salutation

   b. grimace, erosion   **d.** nestle, pollen

Classifying Words

Sort the words in the box by writing each word to complete a phrase in the correct category.

agenda	ambassador	boundary	brambles	coffer
currency	desolate	devour	employ	erosion
expanse	foliage	metropolitan	penury	prominent
republic	rural	sacrifice	sanctuary	thicket

Words You Might Use to Talk About Maps

1. a heavy line to show the _____boundary_____ between the two countries
2. stars symbolizing large, busy _____metropolitan_____ areas
3. population maps that show fewer people living in _____rural_____ areas
4. a wide, blue _____expanse_____ to show the Atlantic Ocean
5. a key showing that yellow is the color of _____desolate_____ deserts

Words You Might Use to Talk About Nature

6. moths that _____devour_____ the leaves on the trees
7. colorful fall _____foliage_____ every year
8. a(n) _____thicket_____ so dense that no one could walk through it
9. plants that protect themselves with long, spiny _____brambles_____
10. canyons created by thousands of years of _____erosion_____

Words You Might Use to Talk About Politics

11. offering _____sanctuary_____ to political refugees
12. items on each party's _____agenda_____
13. meeting with the Canadian _____ambassador_____
14. changing its government from a monarchy to a _____republic_____
15. televised the _____prominent_____ politician's speech

Words You Might Use to Talk About Money

16. exchanging your Mexican _____currency_____ at the border
17. _____employ_____ an accountant to set up the business
18. willing to _____sacrifice_____ wages for health insurance
19. finding good jobs to keep from living in _____penury_____
20. placing the money from the sale into the _____coffer_____

 WORD LIST

Read each word using the pronunciation key.

amplify (am´ plə fī)
consecutive (kən sek´ yə tiv)
consume (kən sōōm´)
disavow (dis ə vou´)
feedback (fēd´ bak)
illusion (i lōō´ zhən)
impression (im presh´ ən)
infamy (in´ fə mē)
intercept (in tər sept´)
neglect (ni glekt´)
odorous (ō´ dər əs)
precarious (pri kâr´ ē əs)
probable (prob´ ə bəl)
qualify (kwol´ ə fī)
rash (rash)
recruit (ri krōōt´)
retain (ri tān´)
stricken (strik´ ən)
tempt (tempt)
testament (tes´ tə mənt)

 **WORD STUDY**

Prefixes

The prefix *inter-* means "between."

intercede (in tər sēd´) *(v.)* to go between two or more people in order to concile differences

interest (in´ trist) *(n.)* a feeling of having one's own curiosity or attention

interfere (in tər fēr´) *(v.)* to get in the way of; to become involved in the affairs of others

international (in tər nash´ ə nl) *(adj.)* between or among nations

interrupt (in tə rupt´) *(v.)* to make a break in the continuity of; to break off or cause to stop

intersection (in tər sek´ shən) *(n.)* a place where two or more roads meet; any place where something is divided or crossed

Challenge Words

bolster (bol´ stər)
encroach (en krōch´)
incognito (in cog nē´ tō)
pertinent (pər´ tə nənt)
treason (trē´ zən)

■ **TEACHER TIP: See page ix for suggestions on how to use this page.**

Level G

WORDS IN CONTEXT

Read each sentence below to figure out the meaning of the word in **bold**. Use reasoning skills and the remainder of the sentence to help you. Write the meaning of the word on the line.

1. Ben was **stricken** with a bad cold and could not leave the house.

   <u>afflicted or hit with illness</u>

2. Although it seemed quite **probable** that Vikki was telling the truth, Gabriel didn't believe her.

   <u>likely to happen or be true</u>

3. I soon learned that the **odorous** valley was filled with wildflowers.

   <u>having a distinctive smell</u>

4. Brandon tried to **qualify** his remarks about Courtney's haircut, but she would not forgive him.

   <u>to modify</u>

5. The little boy could not **retain** his grip on so many balloons, so he let them go.

   <u>to hold</u>

6. The cruel dictator will be remembered in **infamy**.

   <u>fame as a result of something bad; bad reputation</u>

7. The arrival of so many new people will only **amplify** the problem.

   <u>to make greater, larger, or stronger</u>

8. The trapeze artists appeared unconcerned about the **precarious** nature of their job.

   <u>dangerous because of insecurity or unsteadiness</u>

9. Paul realized too late that it had been a somewhat **rash** idea to sign up for skydiving.

   <u>reckless or hasty</u>

10. It was my **impression** that we were to meet tomorrow, not today.

    <u>an idea or awareness</u>

WORD MEANINGS

Word Learning

Study the spelling, part(s) of speech, and meaning(s) of each word. Complete each sentence by writing the word on the line. Then read the sentence.

1. **amplify** *(v.)* to make greater, larger, or stronger

   We need speakers to _____amplify_____ the music.

2. **consecutive** *(adj.)* following one another in unbroken order

   It rained for three _____consecutive_____ days.

3. **consume** *(v.)* 1. to use up; 2. to spend

   Cars _____consume_____ a great deal of gasoline.

4. **disavow** *(v.)* to deny belief in, knowledge of, or responsibility for

   I wonder if the governor will _____disavow_____ the actions of his assistant.

5. **feedback** *(n.)* reaction to what has been done or said

   Will you give me some _____feedback_____ on my homework assignments?

6. **illusion** *(n.)* a false idea or image of what is real

   The magician's trick was only an _____illusion_____ created by mirrors.

7. **impression** *(n.)* 1. a mark or stamp made by pressure; 2. an effect produced on the mind, feeling, or senses; 3. idea or awareness

   I have the _____impression_____ that they don't do any work over there.

8. **infamy** *(n.)* fame as a result of something bad; a bad reputation

   After she betrayed her country, she lived on in _____infamy_____.

9. **intercept** *(v.)* to stop, block, or interrupt the path of

   He tried to _____intercept_____ the football but failed.

10. **neglect** *(v.)* 1. to fail to give proper attention to; 2. to ignore; *(n.)* a lack of attention or care

    Don't _____neglect_____ your homework just because you have other things to do.

    The garden suffers from _____neglect_____.

11. **odorous** *(adj.)* having a distinctive smell

    He pointed to the _____odorous_____ mess next to the tipped-over garbage can.

12. **precarious** *(adj.)* 1. depending upon uncontrollable circumstances; uncertain; 2. dangerous because of insecurity or unsteadiness

The mountain climber stood on the _____precarious_____ edge of the cliff.

13. **probable** *(adj.)* likely to happen or be true

It seems _____probable_____ that the store will close early today.

14. **qualify** *(v.)* 1. to characterize; 2. to make or be suitable for; 3. to modify

Her education should _____qualify_____ her for the job.

15. **rash** *(adj.)* reckless or hasty; *(n.)* a temporary outbreak of spots on the skin

Please don't do anything _____rash_____.

I have a _____rash_____ from the poison ivy I stepped in.

16. **recruit** *(v.)* to bring in new members; *(n.)* someone who is brought into a group

We're trying to _____recruit_____ new players to our basketball team.

Have you seen the new _____recruit_____ who's a good scorer?

17. **retain** *(v.)* to keep or hold

The team is fighting to _____retain_____ the championship title.

18. **stricken** *(adj.)* 1. hit by a flying object; 2. afflicted or hit, as with emotion, trouble, or illness

They were _____stricken_____ by the shocking news.

19. **tempt** *(v.)* to entice someone to do something generally thought of as wrong

You can't _____tempt_____ me to keep the lost money.

20. **testament** *(n.)* 1. a document recording a person's wishes after death; 2. any statement of strong feeling or truth

Her actions were a real _____testament_____ to her faith in him.

Vocabulary in Action

The words *illusion* and *allusion* are sometimes mistaken for one another. Remember that an illusion is a misleading image, or a hallucination. An allusion is an implied or indirect reference, especially in literature. One easy way to remember the difference between the two words is to use this simple mnemonic device: A is for Allusion, and Allusions often Appear in Art.

Use Your Vocabulary

Choose the word from the Word List that best completes each sentence. Write the word on the line. You may use the plural form of nouns and the past tense of verbs if necessary.

When the trumpet sounded at 5:00 a.m. on the first day of army training, the young **1**, Tom Mans, began to have second thoughts. He wondered if he could ever become disciplined enough to **2** as an army officer. He wondered if he'd made a(n) **3** decision by signing up for four years of service. Was it too late to **4** his commitment? His doubt **5** him. No, now that he was here, Tom was determined to **6** his dignity and breeze through training. He'd gotten the **7** that it wouldn't be too tough.

Any **8** he might have had about boot camp was shattered in the first week. Tom found himself placed in one **9** situation after another, and it was a struggle to keep his nerve. One day he was **10** with a headache after being hit in the head with a volleyball "missile." Tom's job had been to **11** the missile with a rocket of his own, but he had been too slow to fire back.

It was a(n) **12** to Tom's commitment that he never once asked to leave boot camp and go home. He was **13** to leave, it's true, but he did not want to go down in **14** as a quitter. He wouldn't **15** his sworn duty. He **16** his efforts and discovered that it brought great results. In fact, two weeks later, Tom was able to complete the missile drill successfully in four **17** tries. He even grew to tolerate the **18** gym, filled with sweaty recruits.

At the end of boot camp, each recruit received **19** from his or her commanding officer. Tom's officer was proud of him.

"Tom," he said, "I think it's **20** that you have a great military career ahead of you." Tom smiled and felt a great sense of accomplishment.

1. _____ recruit _____
2. _____ qualify _____
3. _____ rash _____
4. _____ disavow _____
5. _____ consumed _____
6. _____ retain _____
7. _____ impression _____
8. _____ illusion _____
9. _____ precarious _____
10. _____ stricken _____
11. _____ intercept _____
12. _____ testament _____
13. _____ tempted _____
14. _____ infamy _____
15. _____ neglect _____
16. _____ amplified _____
17. _____ consecutive _____
18. _____ odorous _____
19. _____ feedback _____
20. _____ probable _____

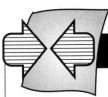 **SYNONYMS**

Synonyms are words that have the same or nearly the same meanings.

Part 1 Choose the word from the box that is the best synonym for each group of words. Write the word on the line.

amplify	consecutive	neglect	precarious
qualify	rash	stricken	tempt

1. unsteady, hazardous, risky   *precarious*

2. lure, decoy, provoke   *tempt*

3. hasty, reckless, brash   *rash*

4. inattention; disregard   *neglect*

5. intensify, broaden, develop   *amplify*

6. disabled, hurt, afflicted   *stricken*

7. characterize, explain   *qualify*

8. successive, continuous, sequential   *consecutive*

Part 2 Replace the underlined word with a word from the box that means the same or almost the same. Write your answer on the line.

illusion	infamy	retain	probable
impression	intercept	consume	

9. Why does everyone have the <u>notion</u> that I don't like to ski?   *impression*

10. Jack tried to <u>seize</u> the message before it got to Mia.   *intercept*

11. Every time we have a heat wave, the air conditioners <u>drain</u> nearly all of the city's electricity.   *consume*

12. It is <u>presumed</u> that the new law will pass.   *probable*

13. I don't know how long she'll <u>maintain</u> her reputation as the best chess player.   *retain*

14. His terrible deeds brought <u>dishonor</u> to his hometown.   *infamy*

15. That great lake in the desert was only a <u>mirage</u>. _____illusion_____

ANTONYMS

Antonyms are words that have opposite or nearly opposite meanings.

Part 1 Choose the word from the box that is the best antonym for each group of words. Write the word on the line.

> consume   disavow   illusion   precarious   rash

1. reality, actuality, truth   _____illusion_____

2. acknowledge, admit, claim   _____disavow_____

3. secure, dependable, safe   _____precarious_____

4. collect, gather, save   _____consume_____

5. thoughtful, deliberate, planned   _____rash_____

Part 2 Replace the underlined word with a word from the box that means the opposite or almost the opposite. Write your answer on the line.

> amplify   retain   neglect   consecutive   infamy

6. After years of <u>consideration</u>, they chose to resolve the issue. _____neglect_____

7. We performed the play on four <u>separate</u> evenings. _____consecutive_____

8. If you leave now, you will <u>surrender</u> your dignity. _____retain_____

9. Do you want to bring <u>honor</u> to this school? _____infamy_____

10. We've tried to <u>reduce</u> the volume. _____amplify_____

> ### Vocabulary in Action
>
> The word *tempt* first appeared around 1225 as the Old French word *tempter*. This, in turn, came from the Latin word *temptare*, which means "to feel, try out, attempt to influence, test." *Tempting*, in the sense of "inviting," is from around 1596. The word *temptress* is from 1594.

WORD STUDY

Prefixes Each of the words in the box combines a form of the Latin prefix *inter-* with another Latin word or root. Read each word history below. Choose the word from the box that matches each word history.

interest	interfere	international
intercede	interrupt	intersection

1. *inter + cedere* (to go)   intercede

2. *inter + natio* (birth; people; nation)   international

3. *inter + esse* (to be)   interest

4. *inter + secare* (to cut)   intersection

5. *inter + ferir* (to strike)   interfere

6. *inter + rumpere* (to burst)   interrupt

Notable Quotes

"If you want to give a message again to the West, it must be a message of love. It must be a message of truth. There must be a conquest (clapping), please, please, please. That will **interfere** with my speech, and that will interfere with your understanding also. I want to capture your hearts and don't want to receive your claps. Let your hearts clap in unison with what I'm saying, and I think, I shall have finished my work. Therefore, I want you to go away with the thought that Asia has to conquer the West. Then, the question that a friend asked yesterday, "Did I believe in one world?" Of course, I believe in one world. And how can I possibly do otherwise, when I become an inheritor of the message of love that these great unconquerable teachers left for us? You can redeliver that message now, in this age of democracy, in the age of awakening of the poorest of the poor, you can redeliver this message with the greatest emphasis."

—Mohandas "Mahatma" Gandhi (1869–1948), peace activist, political and spiritual leader of India (from 1947 speech at Inter-Asian Relations Conference, New Delhi, India)

CHALLENGE WORDS

Word Learning—Challenge!

Study the spelling, part(s) of speech, and meaning(s) of each word. Complete each sentence by writing the word on the line. Then read the sentence.

1. **bolster** *(v.)* to reinforce or give support to, especially in regard to one's spirits

   He tried to _____bolster_____ my confidence, but I still felt bad.

2. **encroach** *(v.)* 1. to enter gradually into the territory, possessions, or rights of another; 2. to move beyond the established limits

   The Sahara continues to _____encroach_____ into formerly green territory.

3. **incognito** *(adj.)* having an unknown identity

   We went to the ball _____incognito_____, disguised as popcorn sellers.

4. **pertinent** *(adj.)* relevant to the current situation

   In your notes, please include all of the _____pertinent_____ details.

5. **treason** *(n.)* to betray, usually as an act against the government

   After Corey was caught, he was discovered as a spy and accused of _____treason_____.

Use Your Vocabulary—Challenge!

Spy Story The imaginary countries of Ohala and Sunesia lie next to each other. They are at peace, but the Ohalans suspect that the Sunesians are hatching a plot of some sort. Use the five Challenge Words above to write a story about the Ohalans' attempt to discover what the Sunesians are planning. Be creative!

> ### Vocabulary in Action
>
> The English word **intercede** first appeared around the year 1578. It comes from the Latin prefix *inter* (between) and the root *cedere* (go). These words form the Latin verb *intercedere*, which means "intervene, go between."

FUN WITH WORDS

Hidden among the letters below are 12 of the vocabulary words from this chapter. They are written backwards, forwards, up, down, and diagonally. Find all the words and circle them. Then choose three words and write sentences for each word on the lines.

1. Sentences will vary. _____

   _____

2. _____

   _____

3. _____

WORD LIST

Read each word using the pronunciation key.

append (ə pend´)
cease (sēs)
constrain (kən strān´)
deftly (deft´ lē)
depreciate (di prē´shē āt)
imprint (*v.* im print´) (*n.* i m´ print)
initiation (i nish ē ā´ shən)
keynote (kē´ nōt)
liquidate (lik´ wi dāt)
matriculate (mə trik´ yə lāt)
octave (ok´ tiv)
overture (ō´ vər chər)
practical (prak´ ti kəl)
quell (kwel)
redeem (ri dēm´)
revenue (rev´ ə noō)
sarcasm (sär´ kaz əm)
scoff (skôf)
studious (stoō´ dē əs)
tally (tal´ ē)

WORD STUDY

Root Words

The Latin roots *voc* and *vok* mean "to call" or "to voice."

advocate (ad´ vō kət) *(n.)* a person who pleads another's case
avocation (av ə kā´ shən) *(n.)* something a person does in addition to one's main occupation; a hobby
evocative (i vok´ ə tiv) *(adj.)* having the power to bring forth or produce, especially a feeling or reaction
vocabulary (vō kab´ yə ler ē) *(n.)* all the words of a language, or those used by a certain person or group
vocalize (vō´ kə līz) *(v.)* to say something aloud
vocation (vō kā´ shən) *(n.)* an occupation or a profession; calling

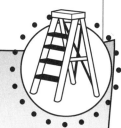

Challenge Words

captivate (kap´ tə vāt)
entail (en tāl´)
infiltrate (in´ fil trāt)
perturb (pər tərb´)
trepidation (trep ə dā´ shən)

■ **TEACHER TIP: See page ix for suggestions on how to use this page.**

WORDS IN CONTEXT

Read each sentence below to figure out the meaning of the word in **bold**. Use reasoning skills and the remainder of the sentence to help you. Write the meaning of the word on the line.

1. A **keynote** of the director's new plan called for 40 new musicians.

   the central idea or part of a speech or program

2. Bobby can **redeem** his prize coupon at the door.

   to turn in and receive something in exchange

3. Jamie **deftly** tossed the pizza dough into the air and caught it with one hand.

   with skill

4. In the fall, I will **matriculate** at the community college.

   to enroll as a student in a college or university

5. Having completed the **initiation**, the members were welcomed into the group.

   the beginning instruction

6. I had to **liquidate** my entire collection of video games in order to buy a new bike.

   to convert assets into cash

7. Kara's wild and reckless behavior is quite different from her sister's **practical** nature.

   having good sense

8. He could no longer **constrain** his feelings of happiness, so Jonas shouted with glee.

   to hold back

9. The **overture** was powerful and moving, but the rest of the musical was mellow.

   an introductory piece of music played by an orchestra

10. We tried to **tally** the votes quickly, but it took us two days to arrive at a total.

    to keep count

WORD MEANINGS

Word Learning

Study the spelling, part(s) of speech, and meaning(s) of each word. Complete each sentence by writing the word on the line. Then read the sentence.

1. **append** *(v.)* to add as an extra part

   We will _____ *append* _____ the chart to the back of the report.

2. **cease** *(v.)* to stop

   Through the negotiations, the two sides decided to _____ *cease* _____ fighting.

3. **constrain** *(v.)* 1. to force; 2. to hold back

   I couldn't _____ *constrain* _____ my emotions.

4. **deftly** *(adv.)* with skill

   She steered the boat _____ *deftly* _____ .

5. **depreciate** *(v.)* to lower in value or price

   The car will _____ *depreciate* _____ in value over five years.

6. **imprint** *(v.)* to produce a mark or pattern on a surface; *(n.)* a mark made by imprinting

   The potter will _____ *imprint* _____ his initials in the bottom of the vase.

   My sneakers left an _____ *imprint* _____ in the sand.

7. **initiation** *(n.)* 1. the beginning instruction; 2. a ceremony to mark a beginning

   We are invited to her _____ *initiation* _____ into the National Honor Society.

8. **keynote** *(n.)* 1. the lead sound of a musical key; 2. the central idea or part of a speech or program

   The _____ *keynote* _____ of his speech concerned the issue of education.

9. **liquidate** *(v.)* 1. to pay off or settle; 2. to convert assets into cash

   Next summer I hope to _____ *liquidate* _____ my debt to my brother.

10. **matriculate** *(v.)* to enroll as a student in a college or university

    He probably won't _____ *matriculate* _____ until the spring semester.

11. **octave** *(n.)* the interval of eight degrees between two musical tones; 2. anything with eight parts

    You are singing one _____ *octave* _____ higher than Margaret.

12. **overture** *(n.)* 1. a proposal or an offer; 2. an introductory piece of music played by an orchestra

    I kept waiting for Mark to make even a small _____overture_____ to peace.

13. **practical** *(adj.)* 1. useful; 2. having good sense

    That's a very _____practical_____ idea.

14. **quell** *(v.)* to stop by force

    I don't know how they managed to _____quell_____ the rebellion.

15. **redeem** *(v.)* 1. to turn in and receive something in exchange; 2. to make up for

    You'll have to _____redeem_____ yourself for the lie you told.

16. **revenue** *(n.)* 1. the income of a government; 2. any source of income

    They will increase _____revenue_____ by raising taxes.

17. **sarcasm** *(n.)* 1. harsh, bitter ridicule; 2. a bitter, mocking, or taunting remark

    Did you hear the _____sarcasm_____ in his voice?

18. **scoff** *(v.)* to laugh at or mock

    I was afraid they would _____scoff_____ at my unusual idea.

19. **studious** *(adj.)* 1. devoted to study; 2. earnestly thoughtful

    This is the result of long hours of _____studious_____ research.

20. **tally** *(n.)* a list or set of marks to keep count; *(v.)* to keep count

    Be sure to keep a _____tally_____ of the donations.

    Did you _____tally_____ the votes?

Vocabulary in Action

Many young people believe classical music is stodgy and boring. But the **overture** to the opera *William Tell* by Gioacchino Rossini appeals to audiences of all ages. The overture's upbeat tempo and grand style have led to its repeated use in the popular media. Most famously, it was the theme music for *The Lone Ranger* radio and television shows of the 1930s, '40s, and '50s. *William Tell* was the last of Rossini's 39 operas, but he continued to compose cantatas, sacred music, and secular vocal music.

Use Your Vocabulary

Choose the word from the Word List that best completes each sentence. Write the word on the line. You may use the plural form of nouns and the past tense of verbs if necessary.

Yesterday my family took my sister to **1** at the Linnover Music Conservatory. Sabrina won a scholarship to the school because of her **2**, hard work and musicianship. Before we left, I **3** a U.S. government bond and sold two old coins in order to buy her a new violin case. Recently, I had read that most of my coins were expected to **4** rather than increase in value. After I **5** the worth of all my coins, I thought it would be **6** to sell some now and buy the gift for my sister. I also **7** a $5 bill to the gift to **8** the debt I owed Sabrina for taking me to the movies last week.

When we arrived at the conservatory, Sabrina was so excited she was unable to **9** her own fidgeting and fussing with her hair. I usually **10** at her nervous vanity, but today I **11** my **12**. Sabrina took us straight to the auditorium for the first-year students' **13**. After everyone was seated, the school's orchestra played the **14** from *The Barber of Seville.*

Sabrina whispered to me, "Do you see how **15** the violinists can finger the notes? One day I'll be able to play that well." Then two opera students sang. I read in the program that one of the singers had a vocal range of almost four **16**. The **17** of the dean's speech concerned the history of the conservatory and its goals for the future. He also spoke of the school's finances and **18** collection. At that point, I **19** listening and thought of Sabrina pursuing her dream.

After the ceremony was over, Sabrina proudly showed us her dormitory. Over the door was a large **20** of the school's motto, "Music for a Living." We helped her get settled and then went out to dinner to celebrate her first step toward a musical career.

1. _____ matriculate
2. _____ studious
3. _____ redeemed
4. _____ depreciate
5. _____ tallied
6. _____ practical
7. _____ appended
8. _____ liquidate
9. _____ constrain
10. _____ scoff
11. _____ quelled
12. _____ sarcasm
13. _____ initiation
14. _____ overture
15. _____ deftly
16. _____ octaves
17. _____ keynote
18. _____ revenue
19. _____ ceased
20. _____ imprint

SYNONYMS

Synonyms are words that have the same or nearly the same meanings.

Part 1 Choose the word from the box that is the best synonym for each group of words. Write the word on the line.

cease	constrain	overture	redeem
revenue	sarcasm	studious	tally

1. proposition, prelude, opening _____ overture _____

2. scholarly, hardworking, industrious _____ studious _____

3. earnings, wages, gains _____ revenue _____

4. score; record, count _____ tally _____

5. quit, halt, end _____ cease _____

6. require, oblige, restrain _____ constrain _____

7. scorn, ridicule, irony, mockery _____ sarcasm _____

8. buy, reclaim, save _____ redeem _____

Part 2 Replace the underlined word(s) with a word from the box that means the same or almost the same. Write your answer on the line.

practical	keynote	append	quell
scoff	matriculate	liquidate	

9. I hope to <u>clear</u> my debts soon. _____ liquidate _____

10. Peter is full of <u>sensible</u> suggestions. _____ practical _____

11. Rachel managed to <u>crush</u> any urge she had to chew her nails.
_____ quell _____

12. He played the <u>first note</u> of the song to help the bond members tune their instruments.
_____ keynote _____

13. When did she <u>enroll</u> at the university? _____ matriculate _____

14. I hope the committee doesn't <u>jeer</u> at my suggestion. _____scoff_____

15. Did you <u>attach</u> the new report to the old one? _____append_____

 **ANTONYMS**

Antonyms are words that have opposite or nearly opposite meanings.

Part 1 Choose the word from the box that is the best antonym for each group of words. Write the word on the line.

append	constrain	depreciate	overture	redeem

1. request, free, release _____constrain_____

2. increase, make valuable _____depreciate_____

3. remove, detach, omit _____append_____

4. lose, forfeit, give up _____redeem_____

5. finale, close, a rejection _____overture_____

Part 2 Replace the underlined word with a word from the box that means the opposite or almost the opposite. Write your answer on the line.

cease	quell	studious	deftly	scoff

6. Sandra has a very <u>negligent</u> approach to her schoolwork. _____studious_____

7. I think he will <u>cheer</u> at your decision. _____scoff_____

8. The runner moved <u>clumsily</u> through the crowd. _____deftly_____

9. When did they <u>start</u> arguing? _____cease_____

10. The mayor is hoping to <u>encourage</u> the violence. _____quell_____

WORD STUDY

Root Words Each of the words in the box has its roots in Latin. Read each word history below. Choose the word from the box that matches each word history.

avocation	evocative	advocate
vocabulary	vocation	vocalize

1. *e* (out of; away; forth) + *vocare* (to call) ___evocative___

2. *vox* (voice) + *al* (pertaining to) + *ize* (to convert into) ___vocalize___

3. *a* (off; away) + *vocare* (to call) ___avocation___

4. *vocare* (to call) + *bulum* (a suffix) + *arius* (receptacles) ___vocabulary___

5. *ad* (toward) + *vocare* (to call) ___advocate___

6. *vocare* (to call) + *tio* (action or state of) ___vocation___

Vocabulary in Action

If you look carefully at the all words in the Word Study list, you will notice that they all have the letters *v-o-c-a* at their root. The root of all these words comes from the Latin word *vox*, which means "voice, sound, utterance, cry, call, speech, sentence, language, word."

CHALLENGE WORDS

Word Learning—Challenge!

Study the spelling, part(s) of speech, and meaning(s) of each word. Complete each sentence by writing the word on the line. Then read the sentence.

1. **captivate** *(v.)* to powerfully hold one's attention

   Her magnificent stories always _____captivate_____ her audiences.

2. **entail** *(v.)* to cause or involve as a result of an action

   If we decide to move, it will _____entail_____ a great deal of work.

3. **infiltrate** *(v.)* 1. to filter or enter through something gradually; 2. to move into secretly and with hostile intentions

   The spy tried to _____infiltrate_____ enemy forces.

4. **perturb** *(v.)* to disturb greatly

   I'm sorry, I didn't mean to _____perturb_____ you with this news.

5. **trepidation** *(n.)* 1. fear, great uncertainty; 2. a tremor

   Joon stood in the doorway with _____trepidation_____.

Use Your Vocabulary—Challenge!

Musical Review You are a music critic and have been assigned to write a review of a recital at the Linnover Music Conservatory. You have been given the opportunity to spend some time with the students before the recital. Use the five Challenge Words above to write an article reviewing the concert and describing the students you meet.

> ### Notable Quotes
>
> "He who carries out one good deed acquires one **advocate** in his own behalf, and he who commits one transgression acquires one accuser against himself. Repentance and good works are like a shield against calamity."
>
> —The Talmud

FUN WITH WORDS

The continent of Artunia has eight countries known only by their numbers. The citizens want real names for their nations and have come up with eight different choices below. Using your knowledge of the chapter's vocabulary words, match the name of each country with the clue that describes it. Write your answer next to the clue.

Possible Names

Scoffland	Liquidatia	Far Studious	Appendia
Imprintia	Tallyland	New Keynote	Octavonia

1. Country 1 has only eight citizens. _____Octavonia_____

2. In Country 2, the inhabitants keep count of everything. _____Tallyland_____

3. Country 3 is the "most important" country. _____New Keynote_____

4. Country 4 likes to belittle others. _____Scoffland_____

5. Country 5 has left its mark on the world. _____Imprintia_____

6. Country 6 is attached to another country. _____Appendia_____

7. Citizens in Country 7 once had to sell their land to pay a debt. _____Liquidatia_____

8. All the universities are located in Country 8. _____Far Studious_____

Create a Culture

Write a fictional paragraph about an aspect of life in one of the countries mentioned above. Be as creative as you like.

Answers will vary.

_____

_____

_____

_____

_____

 WORD LIST

Read each word using the pronunciation key.

barometer (bə rom´ i tər)
biology (bī ol´ ə jē)
clone (klōn)
cylinder (sil´ in dər)
evidence (ev´ i dəns)
extinguish (ek stiŋ´ gwish)
fume (fyo͞om)
immerse (i mərs´)
incision (in si´ zhən)
muffle (muf´ əl)
nucleus (no͞o´ klē əs)
probe (prōb)
productivity (pro duk tiv´ i tē)
realist (rē´ ə list)
refine (ri fīn´)
resistance (ri zis´ təns)
revolutionize (rev ə lo͞o´ shə nīz)
rivet (riv´ it)
rupture (rup´ chər)
specimen (spes´ ə mən)

 WORD STUDY

Suffixes

The suffix *-ize* means "to become or cause to become" or "to act in a certain way."

authorize (ô´ thər īze) *(v.)* to approve or permit; to give authority to
hypnotize (hip´ nə tīz) *(v.)* to put into a trance
mechanize (mek´ ə nīz) *(v.)* to equip with machinery
recognize (rek´ əg nīz) *(v.)* to identify or know something
tantalize (tan´ təl īz) *(v.)* to tease by showing something desirable while keeping it just out of reach
terrorize (ter´ ə rīz) *(v.)* to fill with terror; to cause to become terrified

Challenge Words

circumvent (sər kəm vent´)
eventual (i ven´ cho͞o əl)
intrigue (in trēg´)
pivotal (piv´ ə təl)
unison (yo͞o´ nə sən)

■ **TEACHER TIP: See page ix for suggestions on how to use this page.** *Level G*

WORDS IN CONTEXT

Read each sentence below to figure out the meaning of the word in **bold**. Use reasoning skills and the remainder of the sentence to help you. Write the meaning of the word on the line.

1. In our **biology** class, we have been studying how plants take in water.

the study of living things

2. The cooking cherry juice and steam caused the pie crust to **rupture**.

to break open or burst

3. Be careful not to inhale any of the paint **fumes**; they can be very dangerous.

smoke, vapor, or gas

4. My **productivity** increased dramatically after I started working with a tutor.

rate of manufacturing or creating; effort

5. A polished granite **cylinder** served as a base for the sculpture.

a solid or hollow object with the shape of a tube

6. Some fires are so large that water alone cannot **extinguish** them.

to stop from burning; to put out

7. Kay looks like a **clone** of her twin sister.

a person or thing that is identical to another

8. Danny is too much of a **realist** to believe in ghosts.

one who sees what is true or actual

9. I tried to **muffle** the alarm by putting a blanket over it.

to deaden or silence a sound

10. The nurse had to make a small **incision** in my finger to get the splinter out.

a cut

WORD MEANINGS

Word Learning

Study the spelling, part(s) of speech, and meaning(s) of each word. Complete each sentence by writing the word on the line. Then read the sentence.

1. **barometer** *(n.)* an instrument for measuring the pressure of air

   The _____**barometer**_____ has a very low reading today.

2. **biology** *(n.)* the study of living things

   If you like _____**biology**_____, you might enjoy this film about insects.

3. **clone** *(n.)* 1. a cell or living thing artificially reproduced from another organism with identical genes; 2. a person or thing that is identical to another; *(v.)* to make a clone

   We have made a _____**clone**_____ of the original plant.

   Scientists tried for many years to _____**clone**_____ plant cells.

4. **cylinder** *(n.)* a solid or hollow object with the shape of a tube

   Fill the _____**cylinder**_____ with liquid.

5. **evidence** *(n.)* 1. facts or proof; 2. anything that proves or makes clear

   There is no _____**evidence**_____ to prove your theory.

6. **extinguish** *(v.)* 1. to stop from burning; to put out; 2. to cause to end

   The firefighters tried in vain to _____**extinguish**_____ the blaze.

7. **fume** *(n.)* 1. smoke, vapor, or gas; 2. an angry mood; *(v.)* 1. to emit smoke or gas; 2. to show anger

   There is a great _____**fume**_____ coming from the factory.

   When she heard our decision, she began to _____**fume**_____.

8. **immerse** *(v.)* to cover completely in a liquid

   You can _____**immerse**_____ yourself in the pool.

9. **incision** *(n.)* 1. the act of cutting or carving; 2. a cut

   Rudy made a small _____**incision**_____ in the canvas.

10. **muffle** *(v.)* 1. to wrap in a cloth for protection, warmth, or secrecy; 2. to deaden or silence a sound

    We tried to _____**muffle**_____ the unwanted noises.

    I'm looking for a _____**muffle**_____ for the noisy dishwasher.

11. **nucleus** *(n.)* the central part of anything; core

If you split the _____nucleus_____ of an atom, it will release energy.

12. **probe** *(n.)* an object used to investigate; *(v.)* to explore

The space commission sent a _____probe_____ to Venus.

The explorers want to _____probe_____ the cave for signs of life.

13. **productivity** *(n.)* 1. rate of manufacturing or creating; 2. effort

We are very impressed with the _____productivity_____ of the factory.

14. **realist** *(n.)* one who sees what is true or actual

She'll never go for that strange idea; she's too much of a _____realist_____.

15. **refine** *(v.)* to purify

Those huge machines are used to _____refine_____ crude oil.

16. **resistance** *(n.)* the act of fighting against or opposing

Some people show great _____resistance_____ to new things.

17. **revolutionize** *(v.)* to make major change in

This new computer will _____revolutionize_____ the entire industry.

18. **rivet** *(n.)* a metal bolt or pin used to hold metal plates or other pieces together; *(v.)* 1. to install a metal bolt or pin; 2. to hold one's attention

This _____rivet_____ fell from the pocket of my jeans.

The construction workers will _____rivet_____ those steel beams together.

19. **rupture** *(v.)* to break open or burst; *(n.)* the act of breaking or bursting

With great alarm, I watched the container _____rupture_____.

The collision with the rock caused a great _____rupture_____ in the ship's hull.

20. **specimen** *(n.)* 1. one part of a group; 2. a sample

This is a fine _____specimen_____ of an earthworm.

Vocabulary in Action

The word **barometer** first appeared around the year 1665, most likely coined by the English scientist Robert Boyle. The word comes from two Greek words *baros* (weight) and *metron* (measure).

Use Your Vocabulary

Choose the word from the Word List that best completes each sentence. Write the word on the line. You may use the plural form of nouns and the past tense of verbs if necessary.

Last week, my science class studied the weather and the atmosphere. We even learned to read a(n) **1**. My teacher told us that this week we will study **2** and examine the cells of living things.

"We are going to dissect an earthworm," Mr. Gardner announced. I quickly put a hand over my mouth to **3** my gasp. Then Mr. Gardner continued, "I'd like to **4** any protests you have right away. Your **5** to this assignment is useless. However, I think you will be excited about this lab. Technology has **6** the way you will dissect this earthworm.

"You'll do it on a computer. There's no need to use real worms that have been **7** in a chemical solution." He went on to explain that he thought the computer work would increase our **8**.

My lab partner and I started the dissection program. Several earthworms were displayed on the screen, and we selected one as our **9**. The outside of the worm looked like a long pink **10**. I used a "virtual scalpel" to make the first **11**.

The whole class was completely **12** by the program for the next hour. As Jeff and I **13** the worm's organs, examining its heart and digestive tract, we kept careful notes of the **14** we found. Unfortunately, we accidentally **15** the heart by clicking on it with the scalpel too many times.

With the computer program, we could zoom in on the worm's tissues and see the **16** of a cell. The program even demonstrated how cells **17** themselves to reproduce.

After we finished the experiment, Jeff and I **18** our notes and wrote up our lab report. The bell rang before we finished. Jeff hates homework, so he **19** about having to finish the report at home. I don't have Jeff's attitude. As a(n) **20**, I know that it takes extra effort to produce your best work.

1. _____ barometer
2. _____ biology
3. _____ muffle
4. _____ extinguish
5. _____ resistance
6. _____ revolutionized
7. _____ immersed
8. _____ productivity
9. _____ specimen
10. _____ cylinder
11. _____ incision
12. _____ riveted
13. _____ probed
14. _____ evidence
15. _____ ruptured
16. _____ nucleus
17. _____ clone
18. _____ refined
19. _____ fumed
20. _____ realist

SYNONYMS

Synonyms are words that have the same or nearly the same meanings.

Part 1 Choose the word from the box that is the best synonym for each group of words. Write the word on the line.

biology	clone	fume	immerse
muffle	refine	resistance	specimen

1. life science   _____biology_____

2. submerge, soak, dunk   _____immerse_____

3. defiance, struggle, rebellion   _____resistance_____

4. haze, smog; puff, smolder, rage   _____fume_____

5. enclose, stifle   _____muffle_____

6. cleanse, filter, process   _____refine_____

7. example, model, type   _____specimen_____

8. twin; duplicate   _____clone_____

Part 2 Replace the underlined word with a word from the box that means the same or almost the same. Write your answer on the line.

incision	rivet	extinguish	evidence
revolutionize	probe	rupture	

9. The team will <u>examine</u> the forest for any traces of a UFO. _____probe_____

10. The boiling lava under the earth caused the earth's surface to <u>crack</u>. _____rupture_____

11. He's hoping to <u>reform</u> the hospital system. _____revolutionize_____

12. I see no <u>confirmation</u> that the squirrel was here. _____evidence_____

13. Did you <u>quench</u> the fire? _____extinguish_____

14. She seemed to <u>fascinate</u> her students with the lecture. _____rivet_____

15. There is already a small <u>slice</u> in the pumpkin _____incision_____

ANTONYMS

Antonyms are words that have opposite or nearly opposite meanings.

Part 1 Choose the word from the box that is the best antonym for each group of words. Write the word on the line.

refine	rupture	realist	productivity

1. inactivity, ineffectiveness   _productivity_

2. heal, close; union   _rupture_

3. contaminate, taint, corrupt   _refine_

4. dreamer, idealist   _realist_

Part 2 Replace the underlined word with a word from the box that means the opposite or almost the opposite. Write your answer on the line.

extinguish	muffle	resistance	nucleus

5. I did not expect such compliance from the children. ____ _resistance_

6. All right, everyone, it's time to light the fire. ____ _extinguish_

7. Look through the microscope for the cell's edges. ____ _nucleus_

8. We are trying to amplify the music. ____ _muffle_

Vocabulary in Action

Biology is a branch of knowledge that deals with living organisms such as plants and animals. Did you also know that a biologist is a person who studies biology? One of the more famous American biologists is Rachel Carson (1907–1964). Carson was a trained biologist and a best-selling author. Carson presented scientific facts in a poetic writing style. She made science interesting and understandable to average people. She was best known for her books *Silent Spring* and *The Sea Around Us*. Carson's writing about ecology and the dangers of pesticides was essential to the start of the environmental movement.

WORD STUDY

Suffixes Choose the word from the box below that best completes each of the following sentences.

> authorize   hypnotize   mechanized
>
> recognize   tantalized   terrorize

1. Will the principal _____authorize_____ our trip to the observatory?

2. The delicious goods in the bakery window _____tantalized_____ us as we passed.

3. Did you _____recognize_____ Aunt Julia when you saw her?

4. The rhythmic motion of the windshield wipers began to _____hypnotize_____ her.

5. My little brother tries to _____terrorize_____ me with plastic spiders and snakes.

6. The city has _____mechanized_____ many jobs that were once done by people.

Vocabulary in Action

The word **tantalize** first came from the Latin *Tantalus* and the Greek *Tantalos*. In Greek mythology, Tantalus—king of Phrygia and son of Zeus—was punished in the afterlife by being made to stand in a river up to his chin. Above him were branches laden with fruit that withdrew from his reach whenever he tried to grab them. Similarly, when Tantalus bent his face to drink, the water receded and he was unable to quench his thirst. Thus *tantalize* came to mean "temptation without satisfaction."

CHALLENGE WORDS

Word Learning—Challenge!

Study the spelling, part(s) of speech, and meaning(s) of each word. Complete each sentence by writing the word on the line. Then read the sentence.

1. **circumvent** *(v.)* to strategically get around an object or a situation

   We were unable to _____circumvent_____ the machine's collapse.

2. **eventual** *(adj.)* 1. taking place at some later time; 2. ultimately resulting

   We knew to expect the machine's _____eventual_____ breakdown.

3. **intrigue** *(v.)* to arouse interest or curiosity

   I think that mechanical equipment will always _____intrigue_____ me.

4. **pivotal** *(adj.)* extremely important or crucial

   This was a _____pivotal_____ event in the war.

5. **unison** *(n.)* harmonious agreement or accord

   The students greeted their teacher in _____unison_____.

Use Your Vocabulary—Challenge!

Science Class Journal Your biology teacher intends to have your class dissect a frog at some point. Some students do not want to do this lab and try to avoid it. Use the five Challenge Words above to write a fictional journal entry of your class's attempt to prevent the teacher from assigning this experiment. Be creative!

> ### *Notable Quotes*
>
> "There is a grandeur in the uniformity of the mass. When a fashion, a dance, a song, a slogan or a joke sweeps like wildfire from one end of the continent to the other, and a hundred million people roar with laughter, sway their bodies in **unison**, hum one song or break forth in anger and denunciation, there is the overpowering feeling that in this country we have come nearer the brotherhood of man than ever before."
>
> —Eric Hoffer (1902–1983), writer

FUN WITH WORDS

Use the vocabulary words from this chapter to complete the following crossword puzzle.

Across

5. effort

7. study of life

8. an exact copy

11. a sample

13. to show anger

14. a cut

15. one who sees fact

Down

1. to change radically

2. to inspect

3. the core

4. a hollow tube or container

6. to dunk in a liquid

9. to install a metallic pin

10. to quiet

12. to purify

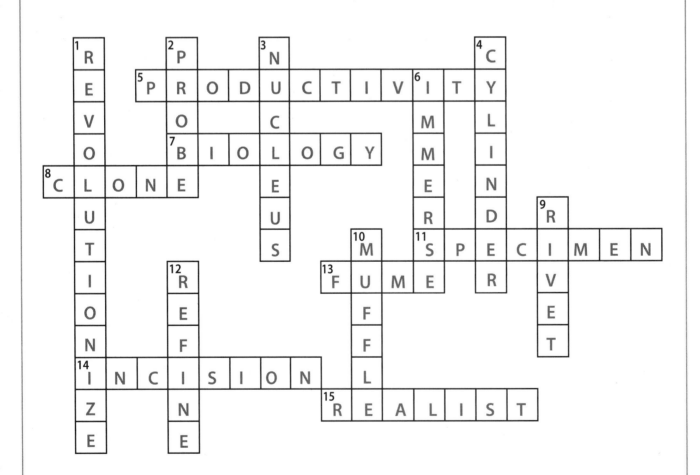

Review 10–12

Word Meanings Fill in the bubble next to the word that best defines each word below.

1. to deplete or use all of
   (a.) consume   (b.) retain   (c.) depreciate   (d.) tempt

2. likely to occur
   (a.) stricken   **(b.)** probable   (c.) practical   (d.) precarious

3. a device that measures atmospheric pressure
   (a.) feedback   (b.) cylinder   **(c.)** barometer   (d.) biology

4. a bad reputation
   (a.) evidence   **(b.)** infamy   (c.) sarcasm   (d.) illusion

5. to attach an additional part
   (a.) rivet   (b.) probe   (c.) cease   **(d.)** append

6. to produce an exact copy of
   (a.) clone   (b.) liquidate   (c.) quell   (d.) immerse

7. a tool used to explore or examine
   (a.) productivity   (b.) nucleus   (c.) specimen   **(d.)** probe

8. marked by a steady attention to learning
   (a.) probable   (b.) odorous   **(c.)** studious   (d.) consecutive

9. to purify
   (a.) extinguish   **(b.)** refine   (c.) neglect   (d.) disavow

10. with quickness and sureness
    (a.) rash   **(b.)** deftly   (c.) tally   (d.) realist

11. to continue to possess
    (a.) retain   (b.) matriculate   (c.) intercept   (d.) qualify

12. a response to something said
    (a.) barometer   (b.) impression   (c.) rupture   **(d.)** feedback

13. to make a mark on a surface by pressing
    (a.) constrain   (b.) revolutionize   **(c.)** imprint   (d.) consume

14. something that supports or illustrates
    (a.) evidence   (b.) keynote   (c.) illusion   (d.) initiation

15. having a definite smell
    (a.) practical   **(b.)** odorous   (c.) stricken   (d.) studious

16. a tone that is eight full tones above or below another
    (a.) muffle   (b.) sarcasm   (c.) overture   **(d.)** octave

17. opposition to something
    (a.) realist   (b.) infamy   **(c.)** resistance   (d.) incision

18. to put down forcibly
(a.) cease   (b.) fume   (c.) quell   (d.) redeem

19. money taken in
(a.) recruit   (b.) keynote   (c.) testament   (d.) revenue

20. to make fit
(a.) qualify   (b.) scoff   (c.) stricken   (d.) amplify

Sentence Completion Choose the word from the box that best completes each of the following sentences. Write the word in the blank.

tally	fume	immersed	recruit	practical
precarious	nucleus	consecutive	neglect	scoffed

1. The _____nucleus_____ of the old building remained intact even after the fire.

2. Bill's classmates _____scoffed_____ at his idea of building a paper-clip computer.

3. If you _____neglect_____ your studies, your grades will slip.

4. The swimmers _____immersed_____ themselves in the cool waters of the lake.

5. Joshua had to admit that keeping a large dog in his one-room apartment was not _____practical_____.

6. Holly continued to _____fume_____ silently about her argument with Paul.

7. We're trying to _____recruit_____ people to join our choir.

8. The final _____tally_____ showed that Mitch had won the contest.

9. It has rained for six _____consecutive_____ days.

10. Jason's _____precarious_____ tree house finally blew down in the storm.

Fill in the Blanks Fill in the bubble of the pair of words that best completes each sentence.

1. The scientist worked for years to _____ the process she used to _____ rare plants.
(a.) immerse, tally   (c.) refine, clone
(b.) extinguish, rivet   (d.) consume, cease

2. You may _____ at my strict study schedule, but it increases my _____ and gives me more free time in the long run.

   a. disavow, feedback   **c.** scoff, productivity

   b. matriculate, evidence   **d.** revolutionize, neglect

3. The _____ gave _____ that the air pressure was rising.

   a. barometer, evidence   **c.** sarcasm, revenue

   b. recruit, octave   **d.** imprint, resistance

4. The scenery helped the actor give the _____ that she was in a(n) _____ position.

   a. testament, practical   **c.** incision, stricken

   b. evidence, studious   **d.** impression, precarious

5. As soon as he had made the _____ statement, Larry wished he could _____ it.

   a. studious, qualify   **c.** odorous, amplify

   b. rash, disavow   **d.** practical, extinguish

6. The new _____ worked hard to _____ for a promotion.

   a. infamy, tempt   **c.** nucleus, scoff

   b. recruit, qualify   **d.** overture, intercept

7. After the program, the _____ speaker asked a few people for _____ about his ideas.

   a. probable, revenue   **c.** keynote, feedback

   b. stricken, sarcasm   **d.** studious, resistance

8. The chef _____ the potholder in water to _____ the flames.

   a. ceased, constrain   **c.** liquidated, revolutionize

   b. consumed, muffle   **d.** immersed, extinguish

9. The doctor warned that exercising too soon might cause her _____ to _____.

   a. incision, rupture   **c.** illusion, constrain

   b. resistance, redeem   **d.** testament, retain

10. The Environmental Protection Agency _____ diligently to find the source of the dangerous _____.

   a. appended, infamy   **c.** redeemed, sarcasm

   b. probed, fumes   **d.** constrained, octave

Classifying Words

Sort the words in the box by writing each word to complete a phrase in the correct category.

amplify	append	barometer	cease	consecutive
extinguish	illusion	incision	initiation	keynote
muffle	nucleus	octaves	overture	productivity
qualify	revolutionize	rivets	specimen	tally

Words You Might Use to Talk About Clubs and Meetings

1. the _____initiation_____ to induct the new members
2. _____append_____ the new rules to the current bylaws
3. serving two _____consecutive_____ terms as president
4. a speaker discussing the _____keynote_____ of his speech
5. keeping a(n) _____tally_____ as the members pay their dues

Words You Might Use to Talk About Science Experiments

6. being prepared to _____extinguish_____ chemical fires
7. looking at the cell's _____nucleus_____ through the microscope
8. recording data from the _____barometer_____ and the thermometer
9. a collection that shows a(n) _____specimen_____ of each kind of rock
10. being careful when using a sharp scalpel to make a(n) _____incision_____

Words You Might Use to Talk About Entertainment

11. _____amplify_____ the sound so the whole audience can hear it
12. a voice range that spans two _____octaves_____
13. a magician making a(n) _____illusion_____ seem real
14. hoping the performance will _____qualify_____ for an Oscar nomination
15. hurried to their seats when the _____overture_____ began

Words You Might Use to Talk About Manufacturing

16. a machine that can set all the _____rivets_____ in place
17. _____cease_____ production because of a breakdown
18. suggestions for increasing the workers' _____productivity_____
19. using earplugs to _____muffle_____ loud sounds from the presses
20. a new invention that will _____revolutionize_____ the whole industry

CHAPTER 13

WORD LIST

WORD STUDY

Read each word using the pronunciation key.

axis (ak´ sis)
cope (kōp)
illuminate (i loo´ mə nāt)
infinity (in fin´ ə tē)
invoke (in vōk´)
junction (juŋk´ shən)
legitimate (lə jit´ ə mit)
luster (lus´ tər)
minor (mī´ nər)
needle (nē´ dəl)
ornament (ôr´ nə mənt)
primary (prī´ mâr ē)
remnant (rem´ nənt)
remote (rē mōt´)
revolve (rē volv´)
summit (sum´ mit)
swivel (swi´ vəl)
synthetic (sin thet´ ik)
tribute (trib´ yoot)
unattainable (un ə tān´ ə bəl)

Prefixes

The prefixes *super-* and *ultra-* mean "above" or "beyond."

superfluous (soo per´ floo əs) *(adj.)* more than is necessary
supermarket (soo´ pər mär kit) *(n.)* a large grocery store
supersonic (soo pər son´ ik) *(adj.)* faster than the speed of sound through air
ultraclean (ul trə klēn´) *(adj.)* extremely clean, especially free of germs
ultramodern (ul trə mod´ ərn) *(adj.)* extremely modern in ideas, design, and so on.
ultrasound (ul´ trə sound) *(n.)* a sound with a frequency higher than humans are capable of hearing

Challenge Words

comply (kəm plī´)
inverse (in´ vərs)
preclude (pri klood´)
utopia (yoo tō´ pē ə)
wry (rī)

■ TEACHER TIP: See page ix for suggestions on how to use this page.

Level G

143

WORDS IN CONTEXT

Read each sentence below to figure out the meaning of the word in **bold**. Use reasoning skills and the remainder of the sentence to help you. Write the meaning of the word on the line.

1. Is this a **minor** problem that you can solve without my help?

   lesser or smaller in amount or importance

2. Today, many clothes are made from **synthetic** fabrics instead of cotton or wool.

   not found in nature

3. I need to buy a new **needle** and some thread to finish the shirt I am sewing.

   a small, slender sewing tool made of metal, usually used to draw thread through cloth

4. I hope I can **cope** with the triplets when I baby-sit on Friday night.

   to deal with something successfully; to handle

5. After a wash and wax, the car had a beautiful **luster**.

   a bright shine or gloss

6. Thomas has a **legitimate** excuse for being late.

   conforming to accepted rules and standards

7. Our town erected a statue as a **tribute** to war veterans.

   something given or said as a show of thanks

8. My **primary** goal is to finish my science project by Friday.

   the first in importance

9. My mother saved a large carpet **remnant** for my sister to use in her room.

   a leftover piece of something

10. The school is located at the **junction** of Elm Street and First Avenue.

    the place where two things come together

WORD MEANINGS

Word Learning

Study the spelling, part(s) of speech, and meaning(s) of each word. Complete each sentence by writing the word on the line. Then read the sentence.

1. **axis** *(n.)* an imaginary line about which a solid body or geometric object turns or seems to turn

   The earth rotates on its _____axis_____.

2. **cope** *(v.)* 1. to deal with something successfully; 2. to handle

   I don't know how to _____cope_____ with that problem.

3. **illuminate** *(v.)* 1. to provide with light; 2. to explain

   Every morning I wait for the sun to _____illuminate_____ my bedroom.

4. **infinity** *(n.)* 1. unlimited space, time, or amount; 2. endlessness

   The shooting star seemed to shoot out into _____infinity_____.

5. **invoke** *(v.)* to call on for help or support

   Emily will _____invoke_____ the services of an algebra tutor.

6. **junction** *(n.)* place where two things come together

   There was an accident at the _____junction_____ of the two highways.

7. **legitimate** *(adj.)* 1. lawful; 2. conforming to accepted rules and standards

   I'm sorry, but I don't think that's a _____legitimate_____ complaint.

8. **luster** *(n.)* 1. a bright shine or gloss; 2. a reflection of light

   He had polished the wood to a high _____luster_____.

9. **minor** *(adj.)* lesser or smaller in amount or importance; *(n.)* a person under a certain age, such as 18 or 21

   Don't worry yourself over the _____minor_____ details.

   You need your parents' permission because you are still a _____minor_____.

10. **needle** *(n.)* 1. a small, slender sewing tool made of metal, usually used to draw thread through cloth; 2. a long, hollow, sharp instrument used in the medical profession for an injection; *(v.)* to goad or tease

    As soon as the doctor took out the _____needle_____, I got nervous.

    Elliot began to _____needle_____ his sister about her new glasses.

11. **ornament** *(n.)* anything that decorates; *(v.)* to decorate

Have you seen the hood _____ornament_____ on our car?

We decided to _____ornament_____ the room with flowers.

12. **primary** *(adj.)* 1. first in time or sequence; earliest; 2. the first in importance

What is the _____primary_____ reason for this change?

13. **remnant** *(adj.)* a leftover piece of something

I am looking for a _____remnant_____ of blue fabric.

14. **remote** *(adj.)* 1. far away; 2. distant in time or relationship

She called us from a very _____remote_____ location.

15. **revolve** *(v.)* to move in orbit around a center point

During a year, the earth will _____revolve_____ once around the sun.

16. **summit** *(n.)* the highest point of something

The group climbed to the mountain's _____summit_____.

17. **swivel** *(n.)* a fastener that allows an object attached to it to move in a circular motion; *(v.)* to turn or rotate in a circle

I can't find the _____swivel_____ for the base of this chair.

I like to _____swivel_____ in my new chair.

18. **synthetic** *(adj.)* 1. artificial or made up; 2. made of a substance not found in nature

They used _____synthetic_____ materials to make this product.

19. **tribute** *(n.)* 1. something given or said as a show of thanks; 2. an honor or a credit

You are a real _____tribute_____ to your parents.

20. **unattainable** *(adj.)* cannot be gained or found by physical or mental effort

I'm afraid this is an _____unattainable_____ goal.

Notable Quotes

"Hatred paralyzes life; love releases it. Hatred confuses life; love harmonizes it. Hatred darkens life; love **illuminates** it."

—Martin Luther King, Jr. (1929–1968), civil rights activist

Use Your Vocabulary

Choose the word from the Word List that best completes each sentence. Write the word on the line. You may use the plural form of nouns and the past tense of verbs if necessary.

My grandmother is a well-respected astronomer. She wrote one of the __1__ books on the constellations. Astronomy is not astrology, but is an exact, __2__ science of the stars and other heavenly bodies.

Last year a local university paid her a(n) __3__ by naming their new observatory after her. Her studies have led her and my grandfather to many __4__ places around the world. They have learned to __5__ with many hardships while abroad. At the __6__ of her career, she held positions at three universities in different countries. She taught me that ancient cultures would sometimes __7__ the powers of the stars to help them solve problems.

I spent last summer with my grandparents. Every night, I __8__ Grandmother until she let me use her telescope. She taught me how to set it up and gently __9__ it on its base to see the entire sky. She explained that the sky was like a road map. You can find constellations by looking for intersections, or __10__, in the sky. She also explained that the positions of the constellations seem to change as the earth rotates on its __11__. I learned that all the heavenly bodies in our solar system __12__ around the sun.

Once I saw a meteorite, a(n) __13__ of a dying star, falling toward Earth. Grandmother and I talked about the __14__ of outer space. If the universe does have boundaries, what could lie beyond it?

My grandmother says the moon looks like a great __15__ hung to __16__ the sky. The soft __17__ of the moon in the sky is different from any other of the sky's lights. When I was small, she used to tell me that the moon was made by humans out of a(n) __18__ material. At the time, I didn't know she was kidding. When Grandmother was young, people thought that walking on the moon was a(n) __19__ goal.

By the end of the summer, I could list many facts, as well as __20__ details, about astronomy.

1. _____ primary
2. _____ legitimate
3. _____ tribute
4. _____ remote
5. _____ cope
6. _____ summit
7. _____ invoke
8. _____ needled
9. _____ swivel
10. _____ junctions
11. _____ axis
12. _____ revolve
13. _____ remnant
14. _____ infinity
15. _____ ornament
16. _____ illuminate
17. _____ luster
18. _____ synthetic
19. _____ unattainable
20. _____ minor

SYNONYMS

Synonyms are words that have the same or nearly the same meanings.

Part 1 Choose the word from the box that is the best synonym for each group of words. Write the word on the line.

cope	illuminate	junction	luster
minor	swivel	synthetic	tribute

1. unnatural, inorganic, human-made   synthetic

2. praise, recognition, honor   tribute

3. connection, intersection   junction

4. sheen, brightness   luster

5. pivot; pivot, swing   swivel

6. manage, face, live with   cope

7. light, enlighten, illustrate   illuminate

8. secondary, insignificant; juvenile   minor

Part 2 Replace the underlined word with a word from the box that means the same or almost the same. Write your answer on the line.

legitimate	remnant	unattainable	summit
primary	invoke	remote	

9. I think we should adjust our <u>impossible</u> goals.   unattainable

10. How high is the <u>pinnacle</u> of that mountain?   summit

11. My <u>original</u> reason for going is to see my sister.   primary

12. He closed his eyes to <u>summon</u> his ancestors.   invoke

13. Kala is the <u>proper</u> owner of the bicycle.   legitimate

14. I'm just looking for some <u>fragment</u> of my former life here.   remnant

15. They have moved to a <u>secluded</u> village.   remote

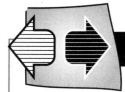

ANTONYMS

Antonyms are words that have opposite or nearly opposite meanings.

Part 1 Choose the word from the box that is the best antonym for each group of words. Write the word on the line.

| cope | remote | legitimate | luster | primary |

1. illegal, improper, incorrect   _____legitimate_____

2. dullness, dimness   _____luster_____

3. following, later   _____primary_____

4. mismanage   _____cope_____

5. close, connected, near   _____remote_____

Part 2 Replace the underlined word(s) with a word from the box that means the opposite or almost the opposite. Write your answer on the line.

| summit | minor | unattainable | synthetic |

6. We make all of our clothes from <u>natural</u> fibers. _____synthetic_____

7. I think it sounds <u>feasible</u> to sell a hundred boxes of cookies.
   _____unattainable_____

8. This issue has played a <u>major</u> role in the presidential campaign.
   _____minor_____

9. She has reached the <u>low point</u> of her career. _____summit_____

Vocabulary in Action

Did you know that the words **tribute**, *tributary*, *attribute*, and *distribute* have the same origin? They all come from the Latin word *tributum* (1340). A tributum was originally a "tax paid to a ruler or master for security or protection." The use of *tribute* to mean "offering, gift, or token" dates back to 1585.

WORD STUDY

Suffixes Choose the word from the box below that best completes each of the following sentences.

superfluous	supermarket	supersonic
ultramodern	ultraclean	ultrasound

1. I need to go to the _____**supermarket**_____ for some groceries.

2. They have decorated their living room in a(n) _____**ultramodern**_____ fashion.

3. Some doctors use _____**ultrasound**_____ to test the health of unborn babies.

4. The new _____**supersonic**_____ jet can fly faster than any other.

5. We don't want a lot of _____**superfluous**_____ commentary on our new plan.

6. You could practically eat from the _____**ultraclean**_____ floors in the cafeteria.

Vocabulary in Action

Today, shopping in a **supermarket** is a common way to purchase groceries. But did you know that your great-grandparents may not have been familiar with the modern supermarket? The idea of self-service food stores led to the modern supermarket. The first store of this kind was developed by Clarence Saunders, who opened a Piggly Wiggly grocery in Memphis, Tennessee, in 1916. Saunders received a number of patents for his ideas, and his stores were financially successful. Another early grocery store chain was the Great Atlantic and Pacific Tea Company, or A&P. These stores opened throughout the United States and were common by the 1920s.

Before the creation of supermarkets, customers pointed to the products they wanted and then waited while a store clerk fetched the items from shelves behind the merchant's counter. The clerk also measured each item and wrapped the amount the customer wanted, since products were not individually wrapped as they are today. This made the shopping process incredibly slow and tedious. Think about this the next time you are annoyed by long lines in the supermarket.

CHALLENGE WORDS

Word Learning—Challenge!

Study the spelling, part(s) of speech, and meaning(s) of each word. Complete each sentence by writing the word on the line. Then read the sentence.

1. **comply** *(v.)* to agree with someone's wishes or orders

   If you refuse to _____comply_____ with their wishes, you will be punished.

2. **inverse** *(adj.)* opposite in nature; *(n.)* something of a contrary nature

   You have too many pencils and not enough erasers, but we have the _____inverse_____ problem here.

   The _____inverse_____ of that situation is too much work and too little time.

3. **preclude** *(v.)* 1. to prevent from happening; 2. to rule out in advance

   Jill's absence today does not _____preclude_____ her future participation.

4. **utopia** *(n.)* a place with a perfect government and social order

   The group wishes to create a little _____utopia_____ here on the island.

5. **wry** *(adj.)* 1. cleverly or ironically humorous; 2. contrary; twisted

   My grandfather has a _____wry_____ sense of humor.

Use Your Vocabulary—Challenge!

Interplanetary Story Astronomers have discovered the possibility of life on the planet Jupiter! But they can't figure out how to make contact with these beings, if they do, in fact, exist. Use the five Challenge Words above to write a story about the scientists' attempts to contact and learn more about the Jupitrons.

> ### Notable Quotes
>
> "Literature is my **utopia**. Here I am not disenfranchised. No barrier of the senses shuts me out from the sweet, gracious discourses of my book friends. They talk to me without embarrassment or awkwardness."
>
> —Helen Keller (1880–1968), author, activist

FUN WITH WORDS

You are a famous astronomer being interviewed for the newspaper. Answer each interview question below using at least one vocabulary word from this chapter. Be sure to answer in complete sentences.

1. When did you first become interested in being an astronomer?

   Answers will vary.

   _____

   _____

2. What do you find most fascinating about astronomy?

   _____

   _____

   _____

3. What discoveries do you think will be made in the near future?

   _____

   _____

   _____

4. Would you like to journey into space? Why or why not?

   _____

   _____

   _____

5. What advice would you give to young people who are interested in astronomy?

   _____

   _____

   _____

WORD LIST

Read each word using the pronunciation key.

authentic (ô then´ tik)
clandestine (klan des´ tin)
demolish (di mol´ ish)
enable (en ā´ bəl)
exterior (ek stēr´ ē ər)
hazardous (haz´ ər dəs)
hefty (hef´ tē)
illiterate (il lit´ ər it)
immense (i mens´)
inferior (in fēr´ ē ər)
jamb (jam)
latch (lach)
notch (noch)
overhang (ō´ vər haŋ)
renovate (ren´ ə vāt)
replica (rep´ li kə)
shambles (sham´ bəls)
usurp (yoo sərp´)
venturous (ven´ chər əs)
verify (vâr´ ə fī)

WORD STUDY

Analogies

Analogies show relationships between pairs of words. Study the relationships between the pairs of words below.

frog is to **fly** as **cat** is to **mouse**

menu is to **restaurant** as **program** is to **theater**

ring is to **bell** as **beat** is to **drum**.

Challenge Words

congested (kən jest´ əd)
facetious (fə sē´ shəs)
juncture (juŋk´ chər)
premonition (prem ə nish´ ən)
vex (veks)

■ **TEACHER TIP:** See page ix for suggestions on how to use this page.

WORDS IN CONTEXT

Read each sentence below to figure out the meaning of the word in **bold**. Use reasoning skills and the remainder of the sentence to help you. Write the meaning of the word on the line.

1. The broken door **jamb** prevented the closet door from shutting tightly.

the side pieces of a door frame or window frame

2. Please **verify** the spelling of your name.

to prove the truth of

3. A tall, **hefty** man kindly offered to help us carry the boxes upstairs.

weighty; heavy; muscular

4. We stood under an **overhang** to get out of the rain.

something that reaches or juts out over

5. The **exterior** of our tent is water resistant.

outside part or surface

6. Our street was in **shambles** after the hurricane.

complete disorder or ruin

7. Is this an **authentic** diamond or a fake?

genuine or real

8. The snowstorm created **hazardous** conditions for motorists.

dangerous or full of risks

9. It didn't take long for the waves to **demolish** our sandcastle.

to destroy

10. When we were at the art show, we bought a **replica** of a famous Dutch painting.

an exact copy; a reproduction

WORD MEANINGS

Word Learning

Study the spelling, part(s) of speech, and meaning(s) of each word. Complete each sentence by writing the word on the line. Then read the sentence.

1. **authentic** *(adj.)* genuine or real

   This portrait is an _____ authentic _____ work of Chagall's.

2. **clandestine** *(adj.)* done in secrecy, especially with deceptive intent

   They arranged a _____ clandestine _____ meeting at the old schoolhouse.

3. **demolish** *(v.)* 1. to tear down completely; 2. to destroy

   The city wants to _____ demolish _____ that old building.

4. **enable** *(v.)* to make possible

   Bringing our lunch to school every day will _____ enable _____ us to save some money.

5. **exterior** *(adj.)* 1. having to do with the outside; 2. coming from the outside; *(n.)* outside part or surface

   There is blue paint on the _____ exterior _____ surface.

   Jamal decided to stucco the house's _____ exterior _____.

6. **hazardous** *(adj.)* dangerous or full of risks

   There are _____ hazardous _____ materials in the back of that truck.

7. **hefty** *(adj.)* weighty; heavy; muscular

   She gave the wheelbarrow a _____ hefty _____ shove.

8. **illiterate** *(adj.)* unable to read or write

   There are many _____ illiterate _____ people in the world.

9. **immense** *(adj.)* very large; huge

   What an _____ immense _____ house that is!

10. **inferior** *(adj.)* 1. lower in rank, order, excellence, or position; 2. of inferior quality

    The woodworking showed _____ inferior _____ craftsmanship.

11. **jamb** *(n.)* the side pieces of a door frame or window frame

    I banged my elbow on the door _____ jamb _____.

12. latch (*n.*) a small piece of metal or wood used to fasten a door or gate; (*v.*) to close with a latch

I have to fix the _____latch_____ on the gate.

Don't forget to _____latch_____ the gate when you leave.

13. notch (*n.*) a V-shaped cut or groove; (*v.*) to cut a notch or notches

Someone made a small _____notch_____ on the back of this wooden chair.

Did you _____notch_____ this desk?

14. overhang (*v.*) to project or extend over; (*n.*) something that reaches or juts out over

The eaves _____overhang_____ the porch, which is nice when it's hot and sunny.

We keep the grill under the garage _____overhang_____.

15. renovate (*v.*) to restore to good condition

The school is planning to _____renovate_____ the old library.

16. replica (*n.*) 1. an exact copy; 2. a reproduction

In the display case, you will find a _____replica_____ of the original Constitution of the United States.

17. shambles (*n.*) complete disorder or ruin

Jessica left the room in _____shambles_____.

18. usurp (*v.*) to wrongly take the power or rights of another by force

The Countess Jalinda tried to _____usurp_____ the throne but was unsuccessful.

19. venturous (*adj.*) courageous and daring; bold

I don't have such a _____venturous_____ spirit as you do; I'd rather stay here.

20. verify (*v.*) to prove the truth of

We must _____verify_____ your identity before we let you in.

Notable Quotes

"No one can make you feel **inferior** without your consent."

—Eleanor Roosevelt (1884–1962), women's rights activist;
wife of Franklin Delano Roosevelt,
32nd president of United States

Use Your Vocabulary

Choose the word from the Word List that best completes each sentence. Write the word on the line. You may use the plural form of nouns and the past tense of verbs if necessary.

Our family just bought an old house near downtown. It was scheduled to be torn down, but we are going to __1__ it. My mom's training as an architect will __2__ her to plan most of the reconstruction.

She says that it's important to use only high-quality materials for the job because __3__ materials won't last as long. She also insists that workers take the necessary safety precautions when doing __4__ work.

The house was built in 1895 and has been vacant for several years. Making it fit to live in will be a(n) __5__ task. The house's __6__ is in pretty good shape. The only major problem is a rotten __7__ that threatens to collapse onto the front porch.

The __8__ to the front door has been broken, and my brother thinks that criminals may have held __9__ meetings inside, even though it is in a(n) __10__. A(n) __11__ kick would take down any one of the weak door __12__. One door has several __13__ in it, and we think they may have been cut by the previous owners, measuring the yearly growth of their children.

We've learned quite a bit about the man who built the house. He was an explorer and quite a(n) __14__ person. At one point, he tried to __15__ the power of local authorities and set up his own city government. He was a very bright man, but __16__. Instead of going to school, he had been educated in the ways of sailors and the sea.

I found an old coin buried in the backyard, and I'm sure it's __17__ pirate treasure, but my mom thinks it's just a(n) __18__. However, she told me I could __19__ the coin's age by checking with an expert.

I can't believe they were going to __20__ this old house. I'm glad Mom decided to make it our home.

1. _____ renovate
2. _____ enable
3. _____ inferior
4. _____ hazardous
5. _____ immense
6. _____ exterior
7. _____ overhang
8. _____ latch
9. _____ clandestine
10. _____ shambles
11. _____ hefty
12. _____ jambs
13. _____ notches
14. _____ venturous
15. _____ usurp
16. _____ illiterate
17. _____ authentic
18. _____ replica
19. _____ verify
20. _____ demolish

SYNONYMS

Synonyms are words that have the same or nearly the same meanings.

Part 1 Choose the word from the box that is the best synonym for each group of words. Write the word on the line.

enable	replica	notch	overhand
renovate	demolish	shambles	venturous

1. remodel, reconstruct, rebuild   _renovate_

2. duplicate, likeness, imitation   _replica_

3. mess, confusion, chaos   _shambles_

4. ruin, wreck   _demolish_

5. allow, permit, empower   _enable_

6. brave, confident, dauntless   _venturous_

7. protrude, stick out; extension   _overhang_

8. mark, tally; score, nick   _notch_

Part 2 Replace the underlined word with a word from the box that means the same or almost the same. Write your answer on the line.

authentic	usurp	verify	latch
clandestine	inferior	hazardous	

9. This is an <u>actual</u> Civil War uniform. _authentic_

10. They made a <u>private</u> agreement. _clandestine_

11. If you don't look out, the rebels will try to <u>seize</u> power. _usurp_

12. We don't accept <u>substandard</u> work around here. _inferior_

13. We should <u>confirm</u> the address before we leave for the party.
verify

14. The blizzard makes for <u>perilous</u> driving conditions. _hazardous_

15. The front door needs a new <u>bolt</u>. _latch_

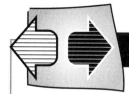

ANTONYMS

Antonyms are words that have opposite or nearly opposite meanings.

Part 1 Choose the word from the box that is the best antonym for each group of words. Write the word on the line.

clandestine	enable	hazardous	venturous	verify

1. safe, secure, protected _____ hazardous _____

2. oppose, prevent, stop _____ enable _____

3. open, plain, public _____ clandestine _____

4. contradict, void, disprove _____ verify _____

5. cowardly, shrinking, timid _____ venturous _____

Part 2 Replace the underlined word with a word from the box that means the opposite or almost the opposite. Write your answer on the line.

authentic	demolish	exterior	inferior	shambles

6. Midge is a <u>superior</u> carpenter. _____ inferior _____

7. The car has a blue <u>interior</u>. _____ exterior _____

8. When I left the house, everything was in <u>order</u>. _____ shambles _____

9. The city chose to <u>build</u> the Thompson Library. _____ demolish _____

10. He showed the police officer a <u>fake</u> driver's license. _____ authentic _____

Vocabulary in Action

One definition of *clan* is "a group united by a common interest or common characteristics." In order to maintain a sense of unity and to protect its common interests, a clan may meet in secret. This may help you remember that **clandestine** means "done in secrecy, especially with deceptive intent."

WORD STUDY

Analogies To complete the following analogies, decide what kind of relationship is shown by the first pair of words. Then fill in the bubble next to the other pair of words that show the same relationship.

1. **sail** is to **ship** as
   - **a.** drive is to car
   - **b.** swing is to sandbox
   - **c.** stop is to bicycle
   - **d.** buy is to groceries

2. **argue** is to **courtroom** as
   - **a.** swim is to exercise
   - **b.** sleep is to kitchen
   - **c.** eat is to dining room
   - **d.** read is to newspaper

3. **intend** is to **accident** as
   - **a.** pretend is to game
   - **b.** expect is to surprise
   - **c.** plan is to vacation
   - **d.** study is to test

4. **citizen** is to **democracy** as
   - **a.** king is to monarchy
   - **b.** dictator is to people
   - **c.** society is to republic
   - **d.** election is to leader

5. **musician** is to **listen** as
   - **a.** singer is to hum
   - **b.** author is to read
   - **c.** architect is to build
   - **d.** mayor is to argue

6. **map** is to **highway** as
   - **a.** road is to city
   - **b.** letter is to post office
   - **c.** calendar is to wall
   - **d.** table of contents is to book

Vocabulary in Action

The word *vex* first appeared around 1415. It comes from the Latin word *vexare*, which means "to attack, harass, trouble." The word *vexation* first appeared around 1400 and comes from the Latin *vexationem*, meaning "agitation."

CHALLENGE WORDS

Word Learning—Challenge!

Study the spelling, part(s) of speech, and meaning(s) of each word. Complete each sentence by writing the word on the line. Then read the sentence.

1. **congested** *(adj.)* to be excessively full or clogged

   The bathtub drain is all ___congested___.

2. **facetious** *(adj.)* 1. comical; amusing; 2. not meant to be taken seriously

   Did you mean what you said about the movie, or were you being ___facetious___?

3. **juncture** *(n.)* 1. a joint or connection; 2. a point in time

   The tire hung from a rope looped about the ___juncture___ of two beams.

4. **premonition** *(n.)* 1. forewarning; 2. a feeling of expectation or fear about a future event

   I had a terrible ___premonition___ about the party on Friday.

5. **vex** *(v.)* to bring distress or great agitation to

   You said that just to ___vex___ me, didn't you?

Use Your Vocabulary—Challenge!

Handy Helpers You and a friend have volunteered with Habitat for Humanity to help paint someone's home. You arrive at the house, and it's a big mess! Everyone will have to do some serious cleaning before you can even begin to paint. This is not exactly how you expected to spend your afternoon. Use the five Challenge Words above to write a story about your afternoon.

Vocabulary in Action

As with many words, separating the prefix from the root can help you remember the meaning of **premonition**. The Latin prefix *pre-* means "earlier than; prior to; before." Monition, the root of the word, means "warning, caution" and derives from the Latin word *monere,* which means "to warn." Combining the two definitions gives you the meaning of premonition— "a feeling of expectation or fear about a future event."

Use at least eight vocabulary words from this chapter to complete the newspaper advertisement below.

FOR SALE
ONE-OF-A-KIND HOUSE

Answers will vary.

 WORD LIST

Read each word using the pronunciation key.

avidly (a´ vid lē)
breed (brēd)
courier (kŏŏr´ ē ər)
disregard (dis ri gärd´)
gallop (gal´ əp)
gesture (jes´ chər)
haunch (hônch)
immature (im ə chŏŏr´)
inheritor (in hâr´ it ər)
naughty (nô´ tē)
quiver (kwiv´ ər)
regard (ri gärd´)
relieve (ri lēv´)
rheumatism (rŏŏ´ mə tiz əm)
scrawny (skrô´ nē)
tempo (tem´ pō)
threshold (thresh´ hōld)
trance (trans)
trough (trôf)
unruly (un rŏŏ´ lē)

 WORD STUDY

Suffixes

The suffixes *-ence* and *-ance* mean "the act of" or "the state of."

clearance (klir´ əns) *(n.)* the act of clearing
confidence (kän´ fə dəns) *(n.)* the state of being confident; self-assurance
entrance (en´ trəns) *(n.)* the act of entering
maintenance (mānt´ nəns) *(n.)* the act of maintaining or keeping in good operation or condition
negligence (ne´ gli jəns) *(n.)* the act of neglecting or ignoring
turbulence (ter´ byə ləns) *(n.)* the state of being turbulent; chaos or disorder

Challenge Words

connotation (kon ə tā´ shən)
finesse (fi nes´)
jurisdiction (jŏŏr əs dik´ shən)
prodigy (prod´ ə jē)
vigilante (vij ə lan´ tē)

■ **TEACHER TIP: See page ix for suggestions on how to use this page.**

Level G

WORDS IN CONTEXT

Read each sentence below to figure out the meaning of the word in **bold**. Use reasoning skills and the remainder of the sentence to help you. Write the meaning of the word on the line.

1. My uncle, a botanist, is trying to **breed** a new variety of roses.

   to cause plants or animals to reproduce and to raise their offspring

2. The company sent a **courier** to deliver the important documents.

   a messenger

3. Robin Hood is usually pictured with a bow and a **quiver** of arrows.

   a case for arrows

4. If a plant is **immature**, it will not bear fruit.

   not fully grown or developed

5. Tea with honey and lemon will often **relieve** a sore throat.

   to free from pain

6. Mom told us to **disregard** the message on the refrigerator.

   to pay little or no attention to

7. We stepped carefully over the painted **threshold**.

   a piece of wood, stone, or metal placed at the floor of a door

8. Is it safe to let my horse **gallop** down the trail?

   to run by leaping

9. As the band played, the audience clapped in **tempo**.

   the speed at which music is played or sung

10. Janine did not remember being put in a **trance** by the hypnotist.

    a half-conscious state, especially one produced by hypnosis

WORD MEANINGS

Word Learning

Study the spelling, part(s) of speech, and meaning(s) of each word. Complete each sentence by writing the word on the line. Then read the sentence.

1. **avidly** *(adv.)* with enthusiasm

   Elliot follows sports _____avidly_____.

2. **breed** *(v.)* 1. to reproduce offspring; 2. to cause plants or animals to reproduce and to raise their offspring

   The people who own the pet store _____breed_____ their own parakeets.

3. **courier** *(n.)* a messenger

   The manuscript was delivered by _____courier_____.

4. **disregard** *(v.)* 1. to pay little or no attention to; 2. to take no notice of; *(n.)* lack of attentiveness or neglect

   Ladies and gentlemen, _____disregard_____ the man behind the green curtain.

   Your treatment of me suggests that you hold me in complete _____disregard_____.

5. **gallop** *(n.)* 1. the fastest gait of a horse; 2. a rapid pace; *(v.)* 1. to cause (a horse or other animal) to gallop; 2. to run by leaping; 3. to move at a rapid pace

   The twins came running at a full _____gallop_____.

   Honey is an old horse, and she can no longer _____gallop_____.

6. **gesture** *(n.)* 1. a motion of the limbs to express or emphasize thought; 2. an action intended to have an effect or be taken as a sign; *(v.)* to make a gesture

   I gave the flowers as a _____gesture_____ of friendship.

   When she's ready to leave, she'll _____gesture_____ for you to follow her.

7. **haunch** *(n.)* the hip, buttock, and upper thigh in humans and animals

   I gave the donkey a pat on his _____haunch_____.

8. **immature** *(adj.)* 1. not fully grown or developed; 2. childlike manner

   Shari grew tired of her sister's _____immature_____ behavior.

9. **inheritor** *(n.)* a person who gains possessions as stated in a will

   I was surprised to be named an _____inheritor_____ in my neighbor's will.

10. **naughty** *(adj.)* 1. disobedient; 2. badly behaved

    Your cousin is a _____ naughty _____ child.

11. **quiver** *(v.)* to shake or tremble; *(n.)* a case for arrows

    I saw his lower lip _____ quiver _____.

    She carried her _____ quiver _____ and bow slung across her back.

12. **regard** *(v.)* 1. to observe; 2. to admire or think highly of; *(n.)* 1. a look or gaze;
    2. respect or esteem; 3. careful thought or attention

    Some people _____ regard _____ this painting with disgust.

    I hold that school in very high _____ regard _____.

13. **relieve** *(v.)* 1. to lessen; 2. to free from pain

    I'm looking for some way to _____ relieve _____ stress.

14. **rheumatism** *(n.)* an illness of the muscles, bones, or joints causing swelling and pain

    My grandmother suffers from _____ rheumatism _____.

15. **scrawny** *(adj.)* thin and bony

    Who would ever believe this used to be a _____ scrawny _____ cat?

16. **tempo** *(n.)* 1. the speed at which music is played or sung; 2. the pace of something

    I think we are playing this piece at the wrong _____ tempo _____.

17. **threshold** *(n.)* 1. a piece of wood, stone, or metal placed at the floor of a door;
    2. a doorway; 3. a beginning

    Brandon stubbed his toe on the _____ threshold _____.

18. **trance** *(n.)* 1. a hypnotic state; 2. a dazed state, as in a daydream

    As she sat in the sun, Maya seemed to be in a _____ trance _____.

19. **trough** *(n.)* 1. a long, narrow container for animal food or water; 2. the gutter at the
    edge of a roof used to collect rainwater

    The pig slurped noisily from the _____ trough _____.

20. **unruly** *(adj.)* difficult or impossible to control

    She had dark brown eyes and a head of _____ unruly _____ red hair.

Use Your Vocabulary

Choose the word from the Word List that best completes each sentence. Write the word on the line. You may use the plural form of nouns and the past tense of verbs if necessary.

A good friend of our family became the __1__ of a horse ranch when her father died. Mary left her job in the city to live on the ranch and __2__ horses. When she was young, Mary rode horses __3__ and won several prizes.

Last week, a(n) __4__ delivered an invitation to my sister and me to visit Mary's ranch. Before we left, our mother reminded us not to quarrel or do anything __5__. She hoped that she wouldn't hear of any __6__ behavior when Mary brought us home. We promised not to __7__ her wishes.

When we got to the ranch, we heard music with a lively __8__ coming through the window. Mary __9__ for us to come in. We walked across the __10__ into a great kitchen. A huge lunch was spread out on the table. "I thought this might __11__ your hunger after your trip," she said.

After lunch, Mary led us out to the stables. My sister became very excited when she saw the first horse. She walked right up to a big, strong horse and patted its __12__. It __13__ at her soft touch.

"You'd never know that Betsy was a sickly, __14__ animal just a few months ago," said Mary. "She was suffering from __15__ and found it painful just to walk. But now she can __16__ like a colt." My sister was in a __17__ as she stroked the horse. I don't think she had even heard what Mary said.

Mary told us which horses we could safely ride. Some were too __18__ for inexperienced riders like ourselves. A friendly-looking gray horse seemed to __19__ me from her stall. She nuzzled my arm when I approached, and I knew I had found a friend. We helped Mary put feed in the horses' __20__ and then went back to the house. I knew it would be a great week.

1. _____ inheritor _____
2. _____ breed _____
3. _____ avidly _____
4. _____ courier _____
5. _____ naughty _____
6. _____ immature _____
7. _____ disregard _____
8. _____ tempo _____
9. _____ gestured _____
10. _____ threshold _____
11. _____ relieve _____
12. _____ haunch _____
13. _____ quivered _____
14. _____ scrawny _____
15. _____ rheumatism _____
16. _____ gallop _____
17. _____ trance _____
18. _____ unruly _____
19. _____ regard _____
20. _____ troughs _____

SYNONYMS

Synonyms are words that have the same or nearly the same meanings.

Part 1 Choose the word from the box that is the best synonym for each group of words. Write the word on the line.

avidly	breed	disregard	inheritor
relieve	scrawny	trough	gesture

1. eagerly, fervently   _avidly_

2. ignore, overlook, disrespect   _disregard_

3. sign, signal; indicate, beckon   _gesture_

4. ease, soothe, comfort   _relieve_

5. puny, lean, gaunt   _scrawny_

6. heir, beneficiary   _inheritor_

7. feed box; chute, channel   _trough_

8. create, generate; bring up   _breed_

Part 2 Replace the underlined word with a word from the box that means the same or almost the same. Write your answer on the line.

courier	regard	quiver	naughty
tempo	unruly	threshold	

9. Mr. and Mrs. Schmidt left the babysitter with six <u>wild</u> children.
unruly

10. Be careful not to trip on the <u>doorsill</u>. _threshold_

11. We sent the package with a <u>runner</u>. _courier_

12. The sight of the full moon caused me to <u>shudder</u>. _quiver_

13. My sisters can be very <u>mischievous</u>. _naughty_

14. This song has a very fast <u>rhythm</u>. _tempo_

15. She doesn't seem to <u>respect</u> his need for privacy. _regard_

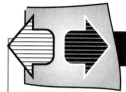

ANTONYMS

Antonyms are words that have opposite or nearly opposite meanings.

Part 1 Choose the word from the box that is the best antonym for each group of words. Write the word on the line.

unruly	scrawny	immature	naughty	disregard

1. adult, developed, full-grown   immature

2. alertness, focus; be mindful of   disregard

3. disciplined, controlled, lawful   unruly

4. well-behaved, good   naughty

5. brawny, hefty, muscular   scrawny

Part 2 Replace the underlined word with a word from the box that means the opposite or almost the opposite. Write your answer on the line.

gallop	avidly	threshold	relieve

6. He read the book <u>sluggishly</u>.   avidly

7. I think the new situation will <u>intensify</u> my anxiety.   relieve

8. She brought her horse to a <u>walk</u>.   gallop

9. We have reached the <u>end</u> of an era.   threshold

Vocabulary in Action

Did you know that the English words **courier**, *occur*, *precursor*, and *concur* come from the same Latin root? The word *courier* first appeared in English around 1382. It came from the Anglo-French *courrier*, which came from the Old French *coreor*. *Coreor* originally came from the Latin word *currere*, meaning "to run." This word is the root for many English words.

WORD STUDY

Suffixes Choose the word from the box below that best completes each of the following sentences. You may use the plural form of nouns and the past tense of verbs if necessary.

clearance	confidence	entrance
maintenance	negligence	turbulence

1. Justin has great _____ confidence _____ in his own abilities.

2. We are responsible for the _____ maintenance _____ of the yard at our apartment building.

3. The airplane passengers experienced some minor _____ turbulence _____ during the flight.

4. Quimby's is having a big _____ clearance _____ sale.

5. The queen made a grand _____ entrance _____.

6. The teacher accused Leila of _____ negligence _____ of her schoolwork.

Vocabulary in Action

Prior to about 1950, the idea of air **turbulence** would have meant nothing to most people. That's because experiencing this "irregular atmospheric motion characterized by up-and-down currents" usually comes from flying in a commercial airplane. Civilian flights weren't available to most of the general public until after World War II, which ended in 1945.

There was a boom in the aviation industry following World War II. The growth was caused in part by manufacturers shifting their focus from the development of military planes to the production of civilian aircraft. The first widely used passenger jet was the Boeing 707, which was cheaper to operate than other early models.

Commercial airplanes began to get much quieter and more efficient in the 1960s. The decade also saw the introduction of solid-state electronics, the Global Position System, satellite communication, and more powerful computers.

Government laws passed in the 1970s allowed for the formation of more airlines. This increased competition among carriers and gave passengers more airlines from which to choose.

CHALLENGE WORDS

Word Learning—Challenge!

Study the spelling, part(s) of speech, and meaning(s) of each word. Complete each sentence by writing the word on the line. Then read the sentence.

1. **connotation** *(n.)* suggested or implied meaning of a word or an object

   The word *immature* often has a negative ___connotation___.

2. **finesse** *(n.)* delicate or skillful handling of an object or a situation

   Let's try to handle this awkward situation with ___finesse___.

3. **jurisdiction** *(n.)* 1. the right to interpret and apply the law; 2. power, authority, or control

   The state has ___jurisdiction___ over the public schools.

4. **prodigy** *(n.)* a person with extraordinary or amazing abilities

   Mozart was a child ___prodigy___.

5. **vigilante** *(n.)* self-appointed law enforcer

   The muggers were caught by a ___vigilante___.

Use Your Vocabulary—Challenge!

Rustling Riders Mickey has been an expert horseback rider since she was six years old. When she was 17, some horse rustlers stole her two favorite horses in the middle of the night. Instead of turning to the police, she vowed to catch the thieves herself. Use the five Challenge Words above to write a story about Mickey and the horse rustlers.

> *Notable Quotes*
>
> "It is only prudent never to place complete **confidence** in that by which we have even once been deceived."
>
> — René Descartes (1596–1650), French mathematician, philosopher

Unscramble the following vocabulary words from this chapter. Then use five of them to complete the business letter below.

1. potme   _____tempo_____   6. grread   _____regard_____

2. rieucor   _____courier_____   7. qruiev   _____quiver_____

3. evielre   _____relieve_____   8. shothreld   _____threshold_____

4. lydvai   _____avidly_____   9. rerdsidag   _____disregard_____

5. turesge   _____gesture_____   10. gourth   _____trough_____

Dear Madam or Sir:

Are you having a hard time keeping up with the fast _____tempo_____ of daily life? Does the thought of driving in heavy traffic make you _____quiver_____? Then hire a(n) _____courier_____ to pay bills, drop off and pick up dry cleaning, and take care of other errands. As an introductory offer, we'll deduct 50% from your first month's bill. If you choose to accept this generous _____gesture_____, call us today. You soon could be crossing the _____threshold_____ to an easier life.

Sincerely,

Good Day Delivery Service

Review 13–15

Word Meanings Fill in the bubble next to the word or phrase that best defines each word below.

1. to break down or crush
   - a. cope
   - b. gallop
   - c. breed
   - **d. demolish**

2. not created in nature
   - a. illuminate
   - **b. synthetic**
   - c. unattainable
   - d. immature

3. to ease or take away
   - a. invoke
   - b. latch
   - **c. relieve**
   - d. breed

4. the very top of something
   - **a. summit**
   - b. quiver
   - c. haunch
   - d. notch

5. second-rate or substandard
   - a. ornament
   - **b. inferior**
   - c. naughty
   - d. immense

6. with great eagerness and interest
   - a. primary
   - b. exterior
   - **c. avidly**
   - d. hazardous

7. at a distance
   - a. venturous
   - b. immense
   - c. hefty
   - **d. remote**

8. a duplicate of the original
   - a. junction
   - b. overhang
   - **c. replica**
   - d. rheumatism

9. a person who delivers something
   - **a. courier**
   - b. inheritor
   - c. minor
   - d. quiver

10. space, time, or quantity without end
    - a. needle
    - b. axis
    - **c. infinity**
    - d. trough

11. to return to an original condition
    - a. revolve
    - **b. renovate**
    - c. notch
    - d. regard

12. having little regard for regulations or standards
    - a. immature
    - b. hefty
    - **c. unruly**
    - d. illiterate

13. a high sheen
    - a. tempo
    - b. shambles
    - c. threshold
    - **d. luster**

14. to confirm that something is valid and true
    - a. swivel
    - **b. verify**
    - c. revolve
    - d. regard

15. to seize power from an individual or a group
    - a. gesture
    - b. renovate
    - c. gallop
    - **d. usurp**

16. lean and gaunt
    - a. hazardous
    - b. authentic
    - **c. scrawny**
    - d. synthetic

17. to overlook or ignore

    (a.) latch   (b.) demolish   (c.) disregard   (d.) enable

18. recognition and appreciation expressed through words or gifts

    (a.) tribute   (b.) jamb   (c.) replica   (d.) trance

19. legal and acceptable

    (a.) primary   (b.) minor   (c.) scrawny   (d.) legitimate

20. to shiver, shudder, or vibrate

    (a.) disregard   (b.) quiver   (c.) verify   (d.) cope

Sentence Completion Choose the word from the box that best completes each of the following sentences. Write the word in the blank.

illuminate	gestured	naughty	clandestine	remnants
unattainable	enable	tempo	shambles	authentic

1. I may be short, but making the basketball team is not a(n) ___unattainable___ goal.

2. The thief's ___clandestine___ plan was discovered by the detective.

3. The band played music with an upbeat ___tempo___.

4. Kevin ___gestured___ for us to follow him down the corridor.

5. The museum will determine whether it is a(n) ___authentic___ Ming vase.

6. Janice's speedy recovery should ___enable___ her to return to school soon.

7. After the party, the clubhouse was in ___shambles___ until we cleaned up.

8. Grandfather said we were ___naughty___ for tricking him, but he laughed as he said it.

9. Although the moon seems to ___illuminate___ the night sky, it does not produce light of its own.

10. Each square in this quilt is made from ___remnants___ of old garments.

Fill in the Blanks Fill in the bubble of the pair of words that best completes each sentence.

1. Television may be the ___ source of information for a(n) ___ person.

    (a.) minor, immature   (c.) remote, naughty

    (b.) venturous, authentic   (d.) primary, illiterate

2. The expert was able to _____ that my aunt's antique bracelet was _____.

   a. illuminate, clandestine   **c.** disregard, legitimate

   b. verify, authentic   **d.** gesture, scrawny

3. The preschool teacher had a sense of humor about her need to _____ daily with a group of _____ toddlers.

   a. gallop, unattainable   **c.** invoke, synthetic

   b. cope, unruly   **d.** demolish, hazardous

4. The _____ dam was built at the _____ of two swift rivers.

   a. naughty, threshold   **c.** immense, junction

   b. minor, trough   **d.** hefty, exterior

5. The earth _____ around the sun and rotates on its _____.

   a. renovates, overhang   **c.** revolves, axis

   b. swivels, needle   **d.** gestures, summit

6. The rebels made a(n) _____ plan to _____ the dictator's power.

   a. legitimate, invoke   **c.** unattainable, regard

   b. clandestine, usurp   **d.** hazardous, enable

7. Brave _____ for the Pony Express _____ through dangerous territory every day.

   a. couriers, galloped   **c.** ornaments, gestured

   b. shambles, quivered   **d.** minors, invoked

8. Before beginning to _____ the old school, contractors had to remove materials that are known to be _____ today.

   a. demolish, unruly   **c.** relieve, remote

   b. latch, venturous   **d.** renovate, hazardous

9. The _____ of the fine china paid _____ to her great-grandmother by using it at every holiday dinner.

   a. threshold, rheumatism   **c.** replica, tempo

   b. inheritor, tribute   **d.** remnant, luster

10. The judge _____ to show which dog she had selected as best of the _____.

   a. quivered, haunch   **c.** gestured, breed

   b. enabled, notch   **d.** illuminated, trance

Classifying Words Sort the words in the box by writing each word to complete a phrase in the correct category.

breed	cope	disregard	enable	exterior
gallop	jamb	luster	naughty	needle
notches	primary	relieve	remnants	renovate
replica	scrawny	shambles	synthetic	trough

Words You Might Use to Talk About Construction

1. ___renovate___ an old house or build a new one
2. a kitchen in ___shambles___ until the workers are done
3. refinishing wood floors to restore their bright ___luster___
4. painting interior and ___exterior___ walls
5. fixing a door ___jamb___ that doesn't hang evenly

Words You Might Use to Talk About Animals

6. obedience classes to train the ___naughty___ puppy
7. ___scrawny___, stray kitten that grew up to be a sleek, handsome cat
8. keeping the horses' ___trough___ filled with water
9. to ___breed___ championship birds as a hobby
10. likes to ___gallop___ the horse through the fields

Words You Might Use to Talk About Arts and Crafts

11. pushing the ___needle___ back and forth through the fabric
12. to make potholders from ___remnants___ as gifts
13. constructing a(n) ___replica___ of the family farm
14. use the ___notches___ to match pattern pieces
15. ___synthetic___ materials that look very natural

Words You Might Use to Talk About Practicing Medicine

16. instructions to see your ___primary___ physician first
17. an operation to ___enable___ the patient to see again
18. teaching people to ___cope___ with crutches on steps
19. not to ___disregard___ good advice about nutrition
20. a nice, hot bath to ___relieve___ pain in sore muscles

Posttest

Choosing the Definitions
Fill in the bubble next to the item that best defines the boldface word in each sentence.

Ch. 13 1. Tania used a **remnant** of the cloth to make a doll outfit for her little sister.
- **a.** yard
- **b.** garment
- **c.** roll
- **d.** scrap

Ch. 5 2. Todd was nervous about the party, so he **lingered** in the doorway before entering the room.
- **a.** remained
- **b.** sat
- **c.** chatted
- **d.** hid

Ch. 12 3. Oil from a well must be **refined** before it is put in our cars.
- **a.** burned
- **b.** drilled
- **c.** purified
- **d.** cooled

Ch. 15 4. Joe awoke from his **trance** when the teacher called his name.
- **a.** feeling
- **b.** tunnel
- **c.** daydream
- **d.** river

Ch. 3 5. At the new club's first meeting, the members **established** the rules.
- **a.** challenged
- **b.** changed
- **c.** abolished
- **d.** set

Ch. 4 6. The remark was said in **jest**, but Darrin took it seriously.
- **a.** amusement
- **b.** anger
- **c.** fear
- **d.** afternoon

Ch. 1 7. The committee is sorry to have to **revoke** the award.
- **a.** accept
- **b.** take back
- **c.** win
- **d.** announce

Ch. 15 8. After winning the local contest, Carrie was on the **threshold** of success.
- **a.** price
- **b.** joy
- **c.** desire
- **d.** beginning

Ch. 11 9. The freshman basketball player handled the ball so **deftly** she was placed on the varsity team.
- **a.** clumsily
- **b.** quietly
- **c.** skillfully
- **d.** quickly

Ch. 10 10. Isabella hoped the teacher would not **intercept** the note.
- **a.** send
- **b.** receive
- **c.** block
- **d.** read

Ch. 6 11. You can avoid the **predicament** next time by planning ahead.
- **a.** enemy
- **b.** illness
- **c.** argument
- **d.** difficulty

Ch. 2 12. Olivia's graphic design business has made her **prosperous**.
- **a.** slender
- **b.** wealthy
- **c.** useful
- **d.** exhausted

Ch. 15 13. If you practice the guitar **avidly**, you can learn to play quickly.
- **a.** rarely
- **b.** lazily
- **c.** often
- **d.** enthusiastically

Ch. 13 14. Becoming a football star is an **unattainable** goal for most of us.
- **a.** reachable
- **b.** professional
- **c.** personal
- **d.** unreachable

Ch. 12 15. Retta looks forward to **biology** class every day.
  a. earth science   **b.** life science   **c.** physics   **d.** chemistry

Ch. 15 16. Many young writers **regard** the famous author as their hero.
  a. look at   **b.** speak to   **c.** listen to   **d.** dislike

Ch. 7 17. Lawrence set out to find the kitten that was lost in the **thicket**.
  a. crowd   **b.** swamp   **c.** shrubs   **d.** maze

Ch. 4 18. Everyone **readily** agreed that Ron should receive the award.
  a. grudgingly   **b.** willingly   **c.** secretly   **d.** enviously

Ch. 3 19. There has been ongoing **opposition** to the proposal.
  a. process   **b.** friendship   **c.** promise   **d.** conflict

Ch. 13 20. The convention will be held in a **remote** region of the country.
  a. popular   **b.** distant   **c.** scenic   **d.** nearby

Ch. 5 21. Many cultures use a **lunar** calendar to measure time.
  a. of the sun   **b.** metric   **c.** of the moon   **d.** different

Ch. 9 22. Mary and her brother often **bicker** over the TV.
  a. exercise   **b.** sing   **c.** quarrel   **d.** work

Ch. 12 23. If you **immerse** the shirt in cold water right away, the stain should come out.
  a. cover   **b.** rinse   **c.** drip   **d.** drop

Ch. 2 24. Every year the anniversary of our town's birthday is filled with **festivity**.
  a. quarreling   **b.** hard work   **c.** dancing   **d.** celebration

Ch. 8 25. The class president gave the formal **salutation**.
  a. banquet   **b.** greeting   **c.** letter   **d.** ceremony

Ch. 13 26. The loud sound made all of us **swivel** in our chairs.
  a. jump   **b.** turn   **c.** fall   **d.** awaken

Ch. 6 27. The tiny sailboat **capsized** in the high waves.
  a. became stuck   **b.** sped through   **c.** turned over   **d.** lost a sail

Ch. 8 28. Before falling asleep, I like to listen to a few **mellow** tunes.
  a. fast-paced   **b.** sad   **c.** relaxing   **d.** loud

Ch. 4 29. The **undaunted** stuntwoman got up and tried again.
  a. bold   **b.** unskilled   **c.** nervous   **d.** injured

Ch. 3 30. The baby ran **blithely** into the house, leaving a trail of muddy footprints on the carpet.
  a. unhappily   **b.** carelessly   **c.** quickly   **d.** hurriedly

Word Relations

Synonyms are words that have the same or nearly the same meanings. Antonyms are words that have the opposite or nearly the opposite meanings.

In the blank before each pair of words, write *S* if the words are synonyms, *A* if they are antonyms, or *N* if they are not related.

1. __N__ overture   keynote
2. __A__ disregard   appreciate
3. __N__ replica   infinity
4. __A__ scrawny   hefty
5. __A__ extol   jeer
6. __N__ inheritor   ambassador
7. __S__ lure   tempt
8. __S__ quell   extinguish
9. __N__ qualify   ornament
10. __A__ rural   metropolitan
11. __S__ righteous   virtuous
12. __A__ cease   prolong
13. __S__ deceive   bluff
14. __N__ obituary   resolution
15. __A__ inferior   premier

16. __S__ mimic   impersonate
17. __A__ verify   disavow
18. __N__ colossal   odorous
19. __S__ incite   provoke
20. __N__ tribute   trough
21. __S__ option   alternative
22. __A__ modest   egotistical
23. __N__ revolutionize   revolve
24. __A__ bungle   succeed
25. __S__ unruly   naughty
26. __N__ incision   exterior
27. __S__ devour   consume
28. __A__ renovate   demolish
29. __N__ infamy   salutation
30. __S__ hazardous   precarious

Using Context Clues

Fill in the bubble next to the phrase that best completes each sentence.

Ch. 9   1.   If you are **nudged**, you may need to
     a. rest for a while.
     b. move over.
     c. find a summer job.
     d. go to sleep.

Ch. 8   2.   You will need foreign **currency** if you
     a. speak a foreign language.
     b. collect old coins.
     c. plan to shop in Paris.
     d. have relatives from another country.

Ch. 3   3.   After Rick's room was **ransacked**, he decided to
     a. paint the room again.
     b. do his own cleaning.
     c. buy curtains.
     d. put a lock on the door.

Ch. 7 4. The dense forest

　　a. was **difficult** to walk through.　　**c.** needed rain.

　　b. was light and airy.　　**d.** was slowly dying.

Ch. 1 5. If you enjoy the **cinema**, you probably like

　　a. spicy foods.　　**c.** fast rides.

　　b. good movies.　　**d.** beautiful scenery.

Ch. 2 6. I felt **blissful** after I

　　a. stepped into the snowstorm.　　**c.** did 100 pushups.

　　b. got the good news.　　**d.** heard the bad news.

Ch. 14 7. You could **renovate** the old bookcase with

　　a. a sledgehammer.　　**c.** paint remover.

　　b. books and records.　　**d.** a cart.

Ch. 5 8. A very long **odyssey** might make you

　　a. change your phone number.　　**c.** worried.

　　b. eager to make up.　　**d.** eager to get home.

Ch. 8 9. A **republic** is often

　　a. governed by its citizens.　　**c.** governed by a king.

　　b. a very private place.　　**d.** a very noisy place.

Ch. 14 10. Sari's **clandestine** meeting was discovered when

　　a. her bicycle got a flat.　　**c.** she changed her mind about the job.

　　b. it rained.　　**d.** she sneezed loudly.

Ch. 6 11. Opera singing takes great skill, but I enjoy the more **facile** hobby of

　　a. mountain climbing.　　**c.** gourmet cooking.

　　b. humming.　　**d.** ballroom dancing.

Ch. 5 12. Jesse's **eccentric** friend

　　a. needs help getting around.　　**c.** is an odd person.

　　b. likes to repair cars.　　**d.** speaks with an accent.

Ch. 1 13. Your **modest** younger sister probably

　　a. moves from place to place.　　**c.** saves her allowance.

　　b. doesn't brag much.　　**d.** likes popular music.

Ch. 12 14. A **rivet** comes in handy when you're

　　a. building a metal shelf.　　**c.** hiking.

　　b. fishing.　　**d.** eating breakfast.

Ch. 1 **15.** If you like **suspense**, you may enjoy
- (a.) being in high places.
- (b.) traveling.
- (c.) reading mystery novels.
- (d.) exploring caves.

Ch. 6 **16.** **Lagoons** are characterized by their
- (a.) rude behavior.
- (b.) mild flavor.
- (c.) long, feathery wings.
- (d.) connection to the ocean.

Ch. 14 **17.** Those **notches** on the wall
- (a.) hold all our dishes.
- (b.) were painted by my uncle.
- (c.) show our heights as children.
- (d.) used to be windows.

Ch. 2 **18.** The director's **oversight**
- (a.) prompted her to get glasses.
- (b.) caused a problem.
- (c.) was from the table at the front.
- (d.) made her successful.

Ch. 7 **19.** **Erosion** is most likely to occur
- (a.) on a table.
- (b.) near a city.
- (c.) in an airplane engine.
- (d.) on a bare hilltop.

Ch. 5 **20.** To study **astronomy**, you will need
- (a.) a telescope.
- (b.) a sports encyclopedia.
- (c.) an interest in buildings.
- (d.) an interest in poetry.

Ch. 4 **21.** If a movie is **overrated**, it
- (a.) is for adults only.
- (b.) sounds better than it is.
- (c.) sounds worse than it is.
- (d.) costs far too much.

Ch. 12 **22.** A forecaster uses a **barometer** to
- (a.) measure rainfall.
- (b.) measure temperature.
- (c.) measure wind velocity.
- (d.) measure air pressure.

Ch. 11 **23.** When objects **depreciate**, they
- (a.) increase in value.
- (b.) decrease in value.
- (c.) disappear.
- (d.) fall apart.

Ch. 13 **24.** If you are on a mountain's **summit**, you are
- (a.) standing on the peak.
- (b.) climbing up the side.
- (c.) at the bottom looking up.
- (d.) walking up a path.

Ch. 14 **25.** An **illiterate** person
- (a.) likes to write letters.
- (b.) reads a book a day.
- (c.) cannot make a speech.
- (d.) cannot read or write.

Analogies Analogies show relationships between pairs of words.

To complete the analogies, decide what kind of relationship is shown by the first pair of words. Then fill in the bubble next to the other pair of words that show the same relationship.

Ch. 6 **1.** **phobia** is to **fear** as
- **(a.)** squall is to wind
- (b.) chill is to heat
- (c.) ocean is to lagoon
- (d.) walk is to crawl

Ch. 1 **2.** **gentle** is to **severe** as
- **(a.)** murky is to clear
- (b.) unkind is to rude
- (c.) scornful is to critical
- (d.) indirect is to lost

Ch. 4 **3.** **pursue** is to **goal** as
- (a.) confuse is to explain
- (b.) indicate is to ignore
- (c.) turn is to change
- **(d.)** narrate is to story

Ch. 5 **4.** **solemn** is to **festivity** as
- (a.) hungry is to meal
- **(b.)** colossal is to pebble
- (c.) heavy is to weight
- (d.) childish is to toddler

Ch. 7 **5.** **boundary** is to **border** as
- (a.) blunder is to correction
- (b.) company is to solitude
- (c.) honor is to disgrace
- **(d.)** prelude is to introduction

Ch. 2 **6.** **abundance** is to **scarcity** as
- (a.) mischief is to trouble
- (b.) virtuous is to good
- **(c.)** harmony is to conflict
- (d.) remorse is to forgive

Ch. 9 **7.** **snoop** is to **meddlesome** as
- (a.) frown is to blissful
- (b.) share is to stingy
- **(c.)** blurt is to unthinking
- (d.) sleep is to wakeful

Ch. 13 **8.** **minor** is to **young** as
- (a.) venturous is to timid
- (b.) drenched is to rain
- (c.) warning is to hazardous
- **(d.)** ocean is to immense

Ch. 5 **9.** **indicate** is to **show** as
- **(a.)** enroll is to matriculate
- (b.) gym is to exercise
- (c.) defy is to enable
- (d.) complete is to unfinished

Ch. 9 **10.** **rampage** is to **violent** as
- **(a.)** tact is to careful
- (b.) thrift is to costly
- (c.) tasty is to delicious
- (d.) trend is to fad

Posttest   Level G

Test-Taking Tips

Taking a standardized test can be tough. Here are a few things you can do to make the experience easier.

Get a good night's sleep the night before the test. You want to be alert and rested in the morning.

Eat a healthful breakfast. Your brain needs good food to work properly.

Wear layers of clothing. You can take off or put on a layer if you get too warm or too cold.

Have two sharp number 2 pencils—with erasers—ready.

When you get the test, read the directions carefully. Be sure you understand what you are supposed to do. If you have any questions, ask your teacher before you start marking your answers.

If you feel nervous, close your eyes and take a deep breath as you silently count to three. Then slowly breathe out. Do this several times until your mind is calm.

Manage your time. Check to see how many questions there are. Try to answer half the questions before half the time is up.

Answer the easy questions first. If you don't know the answer to a question, skip it and come back to it later.

Try to answer all the questions. Some will seem very hard, but don't worry about it. Nobody is expected to get every answer right. Make the best guess you can.

If you make a mistake, erase it completely. Then write the correct answer or fill in the correct circle.

When you have finished, go back over the test. Work on any questions you skipped. Check your answers.

Question Types

Many tests contain the same kinds of questions. Here are a few question types you may encounter.

Meaning from Context

This kind of question asks you to figure out the meaning of a word from the words or sentences around it.

> The smoke from the smoldering garbage made her eyes water.

Which word in the sentence helps you understand the meaning of *smoldering*?

smoke	garbage
eyes	water

Read the sentence carefully. You know that smoke comes from something that is burning. *Smoldering* must mean "burning." *Smoke* is the correct answer.

Synonyms and Antonyms

Some questions ask you to identify the synonym of a word. Synonyms are words that mean the same. Some questions ask you to identify the antonym of a word. Antonyms are words that mean the opposite.

The workers buffed the statue until it shone like a mirror.

Which word is a synonym for *buffed*?

polished   covered

tarnished   dismantled

Read the answers carefully. Which word means "to make something shine?" The answer is *polish*.

When she feels morose, she watches funny cartoons to change her mood.

Which word is an antonym of *morose*?

dismal   agreeable

happy   confident

Think about the sentence. If something funny will change her mood, she must be sad. The answer is *happy*, the antonym of sad.

Analogies

This kind of question asks you to find relationships between pairs of words. Analogies usually use *is to* and *as*.

Green is to **grass** as ——————— is to **sky**.

Green is the color of grass. So the answer must be **blue**, the color of sky.

Roots

Roots are the building blocks of words. Many roots come from ancient languages, such as Latin and Greek. If you know what a root means, you can often guess the meaning of a word. Some words are built by adding prefixes and suffixes to a root. Some words are formed by joining more than one root. Note that the spelling of a root can change. Some roots can stand alone as English words.

Root	Language	Meaning	Examples
aqu	Latin	water	aqueduct, aquarium
aud	Latin	hear, listen	audiocassette, auditorium
bio	Greek	life	biome, biology
cise	Latin	cut	incision, concise
dem	Greek	people	demographic, democratic
dict	Latin	say, speak	dictionary, dictate
fin	Latin	end	finite, finale
grad	Latin	step, go	graduate, gradual
graph	Greek	write	autograph, biography
man	Latin	hand	manual, manuscript
pend	Latin	hang	pendant, impending
scope	Greek	see, watch	periscope, telescope
script	Latin	write	Scripture, postscript
sequ, sec	Latin	follow	sequel, consecutive
spec	Latin	look	spectacle, inspect
voc	Latin	call	vocal, evocative

Prefixes

A prefix is a syllable or syllables added to the beginning of a word. The prefix changes the meaning of the word.

Prefix	Meaning	Examples
anti-	against	antibody, antidote
co-, col-, com-, con-, cor-	with, together	coexist, combine
counter-	against, opposed to	counteract, counterclockwise
inter-	between	intercede, interstate
mis-	badly, wrongly	misunderstood, misbehave
post-	after	postmodern, postpone
pre-	earlier, before	preteen, prepare
sub-, sup-, sus-	under	submarine, subcontractor
super-	above, beyond	supersonic, superfine
ultra-	above, beyond	ultraclean, ultramodern

Suffixes

Suffixes

A suffix is one or more syllables added to the end of the word to change its meaning or to change it to a different part of speech.

Adjective and Adverb Suffixes

Suffix	Meaning	Examples
-able, -ible	capable of being	readable, divisible
-al	relating to	fictional
-ant, -ent	having the quality of	pleasant, obedient
-ive	having the quality of	talkative
-less	without	useless
-ous	full of	joyous

Noun Suffixes

Suffix	Meaning	Examples
-ance, -ancy, -ence, -ion, -ity, -ment, -ness, -ship, -ty	a state of being	vigilance, infancy, turbulence, explanation, generosity, assignment, kindness, kinship, modesty
-ant, -ent, -er, -ist, -or	one who	attendant, resident, hitter, chemist, juror

Verb Suffixes

Suffix	Meaning	Examples
-ate	make	motivate
-en	cause to be	soften
-ify	make	beautify
-ize	cause to be	personalize

Roots, Prefixes, and Suffixes

1. What is a manuscript?

something handwritten

2. What is a spectator?

someone who watches

3. You finalized the plans for your science project. What did you do?

finished them

4. What does an audience do?

listen

5. What kind of things make up a biota?

living things

6. Where do aquatic plants live?

in the water

7. What do things in a sequence do?

follow each other

8. Is something counterfactual true or false?

false

9. What do you do when you liquefy something?

melt it, turn it into a liquid

10. You mispronounced a word. What did you do?

pronounced it wrongly

11. Your front teeth are called incisors. What is their purpose?

to cut into food

12. What is a convocation?

a calling together

13. Who controls the government in a democracy?

the people

14. What can you do with something that is audible?

hear it

15. You want to study one-celled animals. What will a microscope help you do?

see them

16. Where on an envelope would you superscribe an address?

on the top

17. What does a biographer do?

write about someone's life

18. When does a student go to postgraduate school?

after graduating

19. You suspended a piñata from a tree branch. What did you do?

hung it from the branch

20. He predicted that his team would win the game. What did he do?

He said his team would win before the game was played.

21. What is an international agreement

an agreement between nations

22. Your town passed an antismoking law. Describe the law.

It's against smoking.

23. How does a hopeless person feel?

without hope

24. What happens when you sharpen a pencil?

You make it sharp.

25. You are writing a letter. Where do you put the postscript?

after the letter, at the end

26. The inventor activated the robot. What did she do?

started it, made it active

27. The nervous student compressed her lips. What did she do?

pressed her lips together

28. What does an aquifer contain?

water

29. What are coconspirators?

people who conspire together

30. What kind of airplane is an ultralight?

one that weighs very little

Word Cube

Categories: *Partners,*
Visual Learners

Work with a partner. You will each need a sheet of paper, a pencil, tape, and a pair of scissors. Each of you chooses six of the current chapter's vocabulary words and makes a Word Cube. To make a Word Cube, draw six squares in a shape like this on the paper.

Write in each square one of the vocabulary words you chose. Then cut along the outside lines. Fold and tape the sides of the shape to make a cube. Take turns rolling the cubes. To score a point, write a sentence that makes sense, using the two words that were rolled. The first player to get five points wins the game.

Vocabulary Commercials

Categories: *Small Group,*
Technology

Work with two partners. You will need several sheets of paper and a pencil. On one sheet of paper, list the vocabulary words from the current chapter. Then make a list of things you use every day—a bowl, cereal, shoes, and so on. Choose one of the items you listed and write a TV commercial to advertise that product. Write a script that lets all three partners play a role. Use at least 10 of the vocabulary words from the current chapter in your commercial. Practice acting out your commercial. Share your commercial with the class by making a video or by presenting a skit.

Creating Categories

Category: *Small Group*

Find two partners. You will each need a sheet of paper and a pencil. Each partner writes three of the current chapter's vocabulary words that are related in some way. For example, you might list words that are all used to describe people, that are all nouns, or that all describe ways to move from place to place. Challenge your partners to guess the connection between the words you listed.

Conducting Interviews

Categories: *Partners,*
Technology

Work with a partner. You will need a sheet of paper and a pencil. One partner will be a news reporter and interview the other. The reporter writes questions to ask in the interview. The questions should contain at least 10 of the vocabulary words from the current chapter. The person being interviewed answers the questions, using vocabulary words if possible. When the interview is complete, switch places and let the other partner write questions and conduct an interview. If possible, record your interview on audio or video to share with the class.

Crack the Number Code

Categories: *Partners, ELL*

With a partner, write 10 sentences using the current chapter's vocabulary words. Next, assign a number to each letter of the alphabet (A=1, B=2, C=3, and so on). Code all the words in your sentences with the numbers you have assigned. For example, the code for the sentence "The cat sat on a mat" would be the following:

20, 8, 5 + 3, 1, 20 + 19, 1, 20 + 15, 14 + 1 + 13, 1, 20

Once you have coded all the sentences, exchange papers with another group and try to "crack the code." The first team to figure out all the sentences wins the game.

Crossword Puzzle

Categories: *Individual, Visual Learners*

Prepare for the game by bringing to class crossword puzzles from newspapers or magazines. Use these examples as a guide to create a crossword puzzle using the current chapter's vocabulary words. The word clues for "across" and "down" will be the vocabulary word definitions. Use graph paper for the crossword grid.

When finished, exchange puzzles with a friend and complete it. Return the crossword puzzle to its owner to check for accuracy.

Vocabulary Board Games

Categories: *Partners, Visual Learners*

Find a partner and discuss types of board games you like to play. Talk about the object of the game, the rules, and the equipment needed. Then create a Vocabulary Board Game. Think of a way to include the current chapter's vocabulary words in the game. For example, the vocabulary words could be written on word cards. When a player lands on a certain square, he or she must draw a card and define the word.

Create a game board on an open manila folder. Find or make game pieces, and write a list of game rules. Exchange Vocabulary Board Games with classmates and play their games. Keep the board games in a designated spot in the classroom and adapt the vocabulary cards for each new chapter.

All About Alliteration

Category: *Small Group*

Alliteration is the repetition of initial sounds within a sentence. Work in groups of three or four to create alliterative sentences that contain the current chapter's vocabulary words. The only words that can be used that do not start with the initial letter are *and, in, of, the, a,* and *an.* The object of the game is to see which group can come up with the longest sentence. (It can be silly, but it must make sense.) For example, using the vocabulary word *timid:*

> The tremendously timid tiger tossed twelve tasteless trees toward the terrified turtle.

Word Sorts

Categories: *Small Group,*
Visual Learners

Work with a partner. Divide a sheet of paper into four sections labeled *Nouns, Adjectives, Adverbs,* and *Verbs.* Write each of the current chapter's vocabulary words in the appropriate section. When you and your partner feel that you have successfully placed each word in the appropriate box, turn your activity sheet upside down. (Allow only three minutes to complete this step.)

When the time has elapsed, exchange activity sheets with another pair and check for accuracy. (Use your *Vocabulary in Action* book for clarification.) The pair of partners with the most correct answers wins the game.

For an additional challenge, change the part of speech of the vocabulary words by using prefixes and suffixes. For example, if the vocabulary word is *migration,* you could add the verb *migrate* and the adjective *migratory.*

Good News, Bad News

Categories: *Individual,*
Partner

Write a good news and bad news letter to a friend or relative. Alternate sentences that begin "The good news is" with sentences that begin "The bad news is." Use one of the current chapter's vocabulary words in each "good news" sentence. Use an antonym of that vocabulary word in the "bad news" sentence. For example, if the word is *compliment,* you might write "The good news is I received a compliment from my teacher for doing a nice job on my research paper. The bad news is I gave my teacher an insult when I forgot to say "thank you."

For an extra challenge, leave blank spaces for the antonyms and exchange papers with a friend to complete.

Proofread Pen Pals

Category: *Small Group*

Find a friend and work together to write a friendly letter that includes at least six of the current chapter's vocabulary words. Your letter can be about school, sports, friends, family, or any other interesting topic. (Use a resource book to help you with the correct form for a friendly letter.) Include errors in your letter, such as spelling, punctuation, capitalization, and word meaning.

When you have completed your letter, exchange it with another pair of partners. Correct the new letter. After all the corrections have been made, return the letter to the original owners. They will make sure all the errors have been found.

Vocabulary Dominoes

Categories: *Small Group,*
ELL

Begin the game by writing all the current chapter's vocabulary words on index cards. Write the definitions of the words on other index cards.

Place all the index cards facedown in the center of the playing area. This will be the domino bank. Each player chooses four dominoes as his or her supply. Turn one domino faceup to begin play. The object of the game is to match the words with their definitions.

If Player 1 makes a match, he or she places the two cards down on the table, and Player 2 chooses. If Player 1 doesn't make a match, he or she must take a new domino from the bank. If that domino doesn't match either, the player must add it to his or her supply. Player 2 then tries to make a match. The first player to match all the dominoes in his or her supply is the winner.

Impromptu Stories

Category: *Small Group*

Write each of the current chapter's vocabulary word on an index card. Shuffle the cards and place them facedown in a deck. Players take turns drawing five cards from the deck. As each player draws cards, he or she makes up a story using the words on the five cards. Players can use any form of the word listed. To make the activity more challenging, try to make the players' stories build on one another.

Vocabulary Sayings

Category: *Small Group*

Find three partners. Write down the following five sayings:

Birds of a feather flock together.

A rolling stone gathers no moss.

Too many cooks spoil the broth.

A penny saved is a penny earned.

A stitch in time saves nine.

Then brainstorm other sayings. When your list is complete, rewrite the ending of each saying, using a vocabulary word from the current chapter. Example: Birds of a feather sit on our overhang.

Try to create two new endings for each saying. Share your list with other groups or create a class bulletin-board display of your work.

One-Sided Phone Conversations

Categories: *Small Group, Auditory Learners*

Find a partner. Work together to write one person's side of a phone conversation. Use at least 10 vocabulary words from the current chapter. Be sure to include both questions and answers in the conversation. When you have finished, find another pair of students with whom to work. Read your one-sided conversation to the other pair. After you read each sentence or question, ask them to fill in what the person on the other side of the conversation might have said. Then listen to the other pair's conversation and do the same. Try to use vocabulary words as you create the second side of the phone conversation.

Mystery Word Web

Categories: *Small Group, Visual Learners*

Find three partners. Draw a word web on a sheet of paper or on the board. One partner chooses a vocabulary word from the current chapter and fills in the outer circles of the web with clues about the word. The other partners try to guess which word is being suggested. Each partner should take at least two turns describing a word. Be sure to include the Challenge Words in the activity.

Vocabulary Answer and Question

Category: *Large Group*

Gather these materials: poster board, 20 index cards, a list of the current chapter's vocabulary words and definitions, tape. Tape the tops of the index cards to the poster board so that they form five columns of four cards. Under each index card, write a vocabulary word. Divide into two teams and line up in two rows facing each other. Flip a coin to see which team goes first.

The first player chooses and removes an index card, revealing the word beneath it. The team has 20 seconds to provide the definition of the word in question form. For example, if the word *usurp* is revealed, a correct response would be "What is 'to seize power from an individual or a group'?" If a correct definition is given, the team scores a point and the next player in line takes a turn. If an incorrect definition is given, play passes to the other team. The first person in line chooses a new index card. Play continues until all the cards have been removed. The team that gives the greater number of correct definitions wins.

Dictionary Dash

Category: *Small Group*

Find three partners and divide into two teams. You will need a dictionary, a sheet of paper, and a pencil. Write 10 vocabulary words on index cards and place them facedown on the floor. The first team turns over a card to reveal one of the vocabulary words. Each team should then look up the word in the dictionary and record the following

information about the vocabulary word on a sheet of paper:

> how many different definitions the word has
>
> the correct pronunciation
>
> the guide words located on the dictionary page
>
> a sentence that uses the word correctly

When both teams have finished, exchange papers and check for accuracy. The team that finishes first and has no mistakes receives two points. If the other team makes no mistakes, it receives one point. The game continues until all vocabulary index cards have been turned over. The team with the most points wins the game.

Vocabulary Haiku

Category: *Individual*

The word *haiku* comes from two Japanese words that mean "play" and "poem." A haiku is a poem that contains 17 syllables. It is written in a three-line format. The first line has five syllables, the second has seven syllables, and the third has five syllables. Frequently, a haiku describes a scene in nature.

Using the current chapter's vocabulary words, create your own haiku. For example, here is a haiku for the vocabulary word *harmonize*:

> Soft falling raindrops
> Harmonize with the children
> Playing in the rain.

When the class has created several haiku, collect them and create a book. You may also wish to read your poems aloud to the class.

Word Wizards

Category: *Small Group*

Find three partners and divide into two teams. Choose one of the current chapter's vocabulary words. Each pair of partners writes the word at the top of a sheet of paper. The object of the game is to write as many forms of the word as possible by adding prefixes, suffixes, and word endings. For example, using the word *scribe*, you could write these words: *scriber, scribing, script, prescribe, subscription, subscribed, scribed, subscriber, subscript, subscribes, subscribe, subscribing.*

Each round should last three minutes. At the completion of a round, teams exchange papers and check for accuracy. Use a dictionary to clarify any questions.

For each correct word form, one point is awarded. For example, the above list would receive 12 points. Use a new vocabulary word for each round. The team with the most points at the end wins.

Captions

Categories: *Small Group, Visual Learners*

Find two partners. You will need old newspapers or magazines, scissors, paper, and glue or tape. Clip five pictures from the newspapers or magazines. Write a caption for each picture that describes what is being shown. Include at least one vocabulary word from the current chapter in each caption. Attach the captions to the photos and display them in the room.

Vocabulary Charades

Categories: *Small Group, Kinesthetic Learners*

Find three partners. Write on a slip of paper each vocabulary word from the current chapter. Fold the slips and drop them into a box. Partners take turns selecting words and acting them out. The actor may not make any sounds. The first person to guess the word earns a point.

Password

Category: *Small Group*

Find three partners and divide into two pairs. Write on a slip of paper each vocabulary word from a chapter. Divide the slips evenly between the teams. One partner will be the "giver" and the other the "receiver." The giver views the word on the first slip and gives the receiver a one-word clue about it. The receiver tries to guess the word. If he or she is correct, the giver goes to the next slip of paper. If the receiver is wrong, the giver gives another one-word clue. If the receiver does not guess the word after three clues, the giver goes to the next word. The team has three minutes to cover as many words as possible. A point is awarded for each correct answer. The second team then has three minutes to go through its words.

Pledges

Categories: *Partners, Visual Learners*

Work with a partner. Think of ways to improve your school or community. Write a pledge that lists the things you will do to make improvements. Use vocabulary words from the current chapter. Make an illustrated bulletin board of class pledges.

Step Up Vocabulary

Categories: *Large Group, Kinesthetic Learners*

Have the class form a line along one side of the room. Designate a "goal line" about 15 feet away. Ask players in turn appropriate questions about the current chapter's vocabulary words. For example:

What is the definition of (the vocabulary word)?

Use (the vocabulary word) correctly in a sentence.

What is a synonym for (the vocabulary word)?

What is an antonym for (the vocabulary word)?

What is the root word of (the vocabulary word)?

Name three forms of (the vocabulary word)?

What is the present/past/future tense of (the vocabulary word)?

If the player correctly answers a question, he or she may advance one step toward the goal line. The first player to reach the goal line is the winner.

Word Volleyball

Category: *Large Group*

Divide the class into two teams and have them line up facing each other. Toss a coin to see which team goes first. Say one of the current chapter's vocabulary words. The first person on Team 1 must provide a synonym for the word. Then, like in the game of volleyball, the word is sent back to Team 2. The first person on that team must provide another synonym for the word.

Play continues until one team cannot provide a correct synonym. The team that provides the last correct synonym scores a point. Say a new word and continue with the next player. This game can also be played using antonyms.

Class Debate

Categories: *Small Group, Technology*

Divide the class into an even number of teams of four or five debaters. Give pairs of teams the pro or con side of issues they may feel strongly about. For example:

TV has nothing good to offer.

Students should wear school uniforms.

Everyone should learn a foreign language.

Allow 10 minutes for teams to prepare their arguments. Each team must use at least three of the current chapter's vocabulary words in its presentation. Have the teams present their arguments to the class. Have the class choose the winner of each debate. You might make a video of the debates so the students can see themselves.

Listen to This

Categories: *Individual,*
Auditory Learners,
ELL,
Technology

Some English-language learners may be more proficient in oral than in written English. Record each of the current chapter's vocabulary words followed by a slight pause and then its definition. Let individuals listen to the complete recording several times. Then have them listen to each word, stop the recorder, and define the word themselves. They can then listen to the definition to make sure they were correct.

Same and Opposite

Category: *Small Group*

Use this activity for reinforcement or reteaching. Write on index cards each of the current chapter's vocabulary words.

Write a synonym and an antonym for each word on separate cards. Shuffle the synonym and antonym cards and place them facedown on a table. Distribute the vocabulary word cards evenly among a small group of students. One student turns over the first card in the pile. Players must look at their vocabulary words to see if that card is a synonym or antonym of the word on the first card. If it is, he or she takes the card and places it faceup on the table with its matching vocabulary card. Continue until all the cards have been matched. The player with the most matched sets of three wins.

What's the Word?

Category: *Large Group*

Write each of the current chapter's vocabulary words on an index card or self-stick note and display them on a bulletin board. Tell the students to try to use the words during the day. When a student uses a word in an appropriate way, he or she gets to take the card. See who has the most cards at the end of the day.

The following is a list of all the words defined in this book. The number following each word indicates the page on which the word is defined. The Challenge Words are listed in *italics*. The Word Study words are listed in **bold**.

Index of Words   Level G